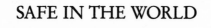

SAFE IN THE WORLD

STUDIES IN JESUS' PRAYER FOR HIS OWN: JOHN 17:6-19

SAFE IN THE WORLD

THE ASSURANCE OF OUR SALVATION

Martyn Lloyd-Jones

Edited by Christopher Catherwood

CROSSWAY BOOKS • WESTCHESTER, ILLINOIS
A DIVISION OF GOOD NEWS PUBLISHERS

Cover illustration: 1987 © Gary Bartholomew.

First printing, 1988

Printed in the United States of America

Library of Congress Catalog Card Number 87-70457

ISBN 0-89107-493-7

All Biblical quotations are taken from
the *King James Version.*

Contents

Preface

1. Our Lord Prays for His Followers: His Reasons and
   Requests   7
2. Not of the World   20
3. God's People   32
4. The Name of God   44
5. The Name of God Revealed   55
6. The Christian and the Truth of God   67
7. Christ Glorified in Us   79
8. Manifesting the Work of Christ   93
9. True Joy   106
10. Kept and Guarded but…   119
11. The World and the Devil   131
12. God's Perfect Will   144

Preface

The sermons in this book form the second part of a series on John 17 which Dr Lloyd-Jones delivered on Sunday mornings in Westminster Chapel between 1952 and 1953. (Subsequent volumes will be published over the next few years.) These particular sermons were preached between April and July 1952, a period when Dr James Packer felt that he was 'on a plateau of supreme excellence'. Many others would endorse that view today, which is why these sermons have now been published.

CHRISTOPHER CATHERWOOD
Editor

1

Our Lord Prays for His Followers: His Reasons and Requests

I have manifested thy name unto the men which thou gavest me out of the world: thine they were, and thou gavest them me; and they have kept thy word. Now they have known that all things what-soever thou hast given me are of thee. For I have given unto them the words which thou gavest me; and they have received them, and have known surely that I came out from thee, and they have believed that thou didst send me. I pray for them: I pray not for the world, but for them which thou hast given me; for they are thine. And all mine are thine, and thine are mine; and I am glorified in them. And now I am no more in the world, but these are in the world, and I come to thee. Holy Father, keep through thine own name those whom thou hast given me, that they may be one, as we are. While I was with them in the world, I kept them in thy name: those that thou gavest me I have kept, and none of them is lost, but the son of perdition; that the scripture might be fulfilled. And now come I to thee; and these things I speak in the world, that they might have my joy fulfilled in themselves. I have given them thy word; and the world hath hated them, because they are not of the world, even as I am not of the world. I pray not that thou shouldest take them out of the world, but that thou shouldest keep them from the evil. They are not of the world, even as I am not of the world. Sanctify them through thy truth: thy word is truth. As thou hast sent me into the world, even so have I also sent them into the world. And for their sakes I sanctify myself, that they also might be sanctified through the truth (John 17 vv. 6–19).

In the first part of our study of John 17, we finished at the end of verse 5.[1] We have seen how this great high-priestly prayer of our Lord can be divided up naturally into three main sections: in the first, verses 1–5, he prays for himself; then from verses 6–19 we have his prayer for his immediate followers, and, finally, from verse 20 to the end we have his prayer for those who would believe on him through his disciples – 'Neither pray I for these alone, but for them also which shall believe on me through their word.'

We have already considered the first section, in which our Lord prayed for himself. It is a great, comprehensive prayer in which we saw outlined and displayed, in a sense, the whole realm of Christian doctrine, as our Lord pleads with his Father that he might grant him grace to go on with the work which he had given him to do, and that he might not fail or falter as he came to the supreme test and crisis, namely, the laying down of his life as a ransom for many.

So now we come to this second section which starts at verse 6 and goes on to the end of verse 19. There has been much debate as to whether in this section our Lord was praying for the apostles only or whether he was praying for all who had believed on him up to that point. It is a question which cannot be finally decided. Those who believe he was praying only for the apostles, the innermost circle, always quote verse 12, in which he says, 'While I was with them in the world, I kept them in thy name: those that thou gavest me I have kept, and none of them is lost, but the son of perdition; that the scripture might be fulfilled.' That seems to indicate that he was talking about the twelve, and saying that he had kept all but one, Judas, who would fail and deny him, according to the scriptural prophecy to be found in the Old Testament. But most of the remaining statements would indicate, I think, a wider circle: those to whom he had manifested his name, all those who had been given to him. He had not only been given the apostles, he had been given all believers: 'Now they have known that all things

[1]*Saved in Eternity* (Crossway Books, 1988)

whatsoever thou hast given me are of thee' (v. 7) and this is something which is true, of course, of every believer. So, in the last analysis, we cannot settle this question any more than we can settle many other questions which are of no final importance. We cannot be dogmatic about it, and this does not matter, because even if the statement is confined to the apostles, it is obviously something that is true also of all who are believers in the Lord Jesus Christ. Indeed, that is confirmed by verse 20, where he says, 'Neither pray I for these alone, but for them also which shall believe on me through their word.' And he goes on, in a sense, to offer the same petition for future believers as he has offered at this point for those who have already believed.

That, then, is just a mechanical, preliminary point. The great matter before us is to observe the terms of the prayer, and it divides itself up very naturally. There are two great things here: our Lord prays for his followers, and he says why he does so. Some would put it as strongly as to say that he pleads for them; he does not merely make requests, he produces arguments and makes statements. In other words, he is giving reasons for praying for them. This is a point which we must surely observe, for it is of great value to us. It reminds us again that God's omniscience is no reason for our not telling him things which he already knows. You must often have found yourself facing a particular difficulty or situation. You feel that because God knows everything, there is no point in telling him anything about it. God knows our need, he knows all about us before we get on our knees to pray, so why then do we need to tell him anything? And the quite obvious conclusion to that thought is that there is no need to pray at all: if God knows all about us, why not let things take their course and all will be well.

Now the answer to that is what we find in this prayer. Our Lord knew, in a way we can never know, about God's omniscience, his perfect and complete knowledge, and yet he told his Father certain things about those disciples, things which God knew already. He prayed about them and repeated them, and, of course, that is characteristic of Bible prayers everywhere, not only the prayers of our Lord but also those of the apostles and of the saints of the Old Testament. This is something which is wonderful the moment you begin to contemplate it. God after all desires us to think of him as our Father. It is a kind of anthropomorphism; it is God stooping to our weakness. The human parent enjoys listening to the child saying things and telling him things which he knows already; he does not resent them, nor does he regard them as a waste of time. He derives great pleasure from them, and we are to learn from this that our heavenly Father delights to see us coming to him, and stating our requests, and giving our reasons. There is an example of prayer in the Old Testament, where that good man, Hezekiah, even takes a letter and spreads it out before God, as if God did not know all about it, and as if to say, 'Here it is, I come to you with this letter and I ask you to take charge of it and to do something about it' (2 Kings 19:14).

So as we come into the presence of God with our requests and our petitions, let us never fear to bring the details, for nothing is too small for God's loving care and attention. He is interested in us as a father is in a child, everything about us is of the greatest interest to him. Read again the Sermon on the Mount and you will find that our Lord says that in an extended form in Matthew 6 where he uses the argument about God clothing the lilies and caring about the birds of the air. Nothing, he says, happens to them apart from God, so how much more is he interested in you and me, and in everything that happens to us, and everything that is connected with the minutest detail of our lives. 'In *nothing* be anxious,' writes the apostle Paul. It does not matter what it is (he uses the most all-inclusive word he could have chosen). 'In nothing be anxious; but in everything' – there it is again! – 'by prayer and supplication with thanksgiving let your requests be made known unto God' (Phil 4:6, RV). Our Lord prays for his people and he adduces the reasons why he prays. Let us ever, as we come to God in prayer, remember his great and glorious example and do the same ourselves.

So I should like first to look at this section, from verse 6 to verse 19, as a whole. There are many ways in which one can approach a passage of Scripture such as this. One way is just to take it verse by verse, verse 6, verse 7, verse 8, and so on, right through. This is a legitimate way of approaching the Scriptures, but it seems to me that a better way, especially with a section like this, is first to look at it as a whole and to extract from it the great principles, and then, having them firmly in our minds, to come back to the details. I have often compared this with the analysis of a great piece of music, which is divided up into movements, each of which may again be sub-divided. It is a great thing to listen to the whole. It is a great thing, too, to listen to these separate big parts and to analyse them. It is much better to do that than to go along thoughtlessly from movement to movement, section to section, and note to note, as it were. So with a passage of Scripture, having got hold of the big principles of the essential teaching, you are able to understand the details in a way that you would not be able to do if you had not started in that manner.

With this section, therefore, I propose to adopt the method we used with verses 1–5. We saw that there were great doctrines enunciated in that first section and we shall find exactly the same thing here. It seems to me that the fundamental division of this passage can again be put in this form: firstly, *why* our Lord prays for his followers, and secondly *what* he prays for them. It is as simple as that. Now if we take the chapter and just read it through, without trying to get at the principles, then there are certain statements here which seem to be rather difficult and almost confusing. But we must realize that there are only these two big things dealt with here: our Lord puts first the reasons why he prays for these people, and then he gives the requests afterwards. Therefore, as we start reading at verse 6 we find a positive statement – 'I have manifested thy name unto the men which thou gavest me out of the world: thine they were, and thou gavest them me; and they have kept thy word.' He makes a categorical statement like that in his prayer because it is only after he has adduced certain reasons that he brings the petition. Of course you find that the two things are really intermingled but for the sake of clarity of thought they ought to be kept separately in our minds as we look at any particular detailed statement.

Let us, then, summarize the first section. Why does our Lord pray for these people at all? Here he is facing his own death, the greatest and the most terrible moment in his life is at hand, and yet he pauses to pray for them. Why does he do it? The answer is all here. He does it first and foremost because of his great concern for the glory of God. While he is on earth, the glory of God is, in a sense, in his hands. He has come to glorify his Father and that is the one thing he wants to do above everything else. And now as he is going to leave these people, over and above his own concern about dying is his concern about the glory of God: it is the one thing that matters.

Secondly, he prays for them because of who and what they are. They are the people to whom he has manifested the name of God; the people who have been given to him; the people to whom he has given the word: people who believe certain things. That is the definition of a Christian and they, and they alone, are the people for whom he has prayed.

Then he prays for them because of their task, because of their calling. He is going and he is leaving them in the world to do something; they have work to do, exactly as he had been given work to do. You see the logic of it all? God sent him, he sends them, and he prays for them especially in the light of their calling and their task – the work of evangelizing. There are other people who are going to believe on him through their word, and so they must be enabled to do this work.

He also prays for them because of their circumstances, the circumstances in which they were placed in the world. He says that they are going to have trouble in the world: 'I have given them thy word; and the world hath hated them, because they are not of the world, even as I am not of the world' (v. 14). There is an antagonism to the Christian in this world – the Bible constantly tells us that the world hates a Christian as it hated his Lord. The apostle Paul reminds Timothy of this. Timothy is frightened because he is being persecuted. He cannot understand it, but Paul tells him that 'all that live godly in Christ Jesus shall suffer persecution' (2 Tim 3:12). Our Lord says the same thing in John 15: 'The servant is not greater than his lord. If they have persecuted me, they will also persecute you' (v. 20), and again: 'If they have called the master of the house Beelzebub, how much more shall they call them of his household?' (Mt 10:25).

That is the argument here. He is thinking of these people in this gainsaying, contradictory world, and because he knows what they are going to endure, he prays for them. He knows the persecution which follows inevitably, in some shape or form, whenever anybody becomes a Christian. It does not always mean that we will be thrown into prison or a concentration camp, or molested in a physical sense, but as certainly as we become like the Lord Jesus Christ we will have to suffer for it – 'We must through much tribulation enter the kingdom of God' (Acts 14:22). Persecution can be very subtle – a mere glance from one person to another, the faintest suspicion of a smile or a curl of the lip, some little indignity thrust upon you – it manifests itself in a thousand and one ways. The astounding thing is that though we are told to be prepared for it, so often when we receive it, we are taken by surprise and wonder why it happens. Do not expect, my friend, that the whole world will rejoice if you become a Christian. You will probably receive enmity and hatred and persecution from certain people. It happened in the case of our blessed Lord, and his followers must always be ready to meet it.

But the last reason he seems to adduce here for praying for these people is that he is anxious that his own joy may be fulfilled in them. We must not stop at what I have just been saying. Our Lord was a man of sorrows and acquainted with grief, he was condemned and crucified on a cross, yet the author of the epistle to the Hebrews says, 'Who *for the joy that was set before him* endured the cross, despising the shame...' (Heb 12:2). There was a fundamental joy deeper than all the suffering, deeper than all he endured by way of the contradiction of sinners against himself, and he was anxious that his followers might know this. He wanted them to experience his own peace, his own inimitable joy. This is possible for any Christian, in spite of all I have said, and in spite of the world in which we live. So if we are not experiencing this joy as something deeper than all these other experiences, then, to that extent, we are failing in our discipleship.

Then, secondly, let me summarize *what* he prays for them. The primary object of his prayer is not so much that they may be one with one another, as that they may be kept in true unity with him, with God the Father, and therefore with each other. That is the nature of the communion. Obviously this has to be worked out in greater detail, and never perhaps was this more necessary than today. This is a chapter which has been much misquoted and misinterpreted, so we must be clear as to what exactly this prayer for unity among believers really is; our Lord does pray for them in that context, and he goes on repeating it.

The next thing he prays for them is that they may be kept from the evil one – the devil, the god of this world, the prince of the power of the air – and the evil that is in the world as the result of his activities and efforts. Our Lord does not pray that they may be taken out of the world – we sometimes wish we could pray that, the idea of monasticism is somewhere down in the depths of all of us. We want to retire out of the world and arrive in some magic circle where nothing can disturb us. There is a longing in the suffering, persecuted Christian to get out of the world. But our Lord does not pray that they may be taken out of the world in any sense, nor that they may be taken out of it by death, but rather that in it they may be kept from the evil. Your business and mine as Christian people is to be in the midst of this world and its affairs, and still remain true and loyal to God, and be kept from the evil. 'Pure religion and undefiled before God and the Father is this,' says James, not to retire out of every vocation in life, but rather, 'To visit the fatherless and widows in their affliction, and to keep himself unspotted from the world' (Jas 1:27). What a glorious but tremendous task it is! And of course it is much more difficult than segregating yourself and going away to live in seclusion and isolation. The task of the Christian is to be right in the midst of this world and its affairs in order that he may do this work of evangelism, spreading the gospel and the kingdom of God, while the whole time, keeping himself unspotted from the world. Christ prays that his followers may be kept unspotted, that they may not be harmed and tarnished and polluted by the evil world in which they find themselves. It is a glorious task.

And his last petition is that they may be sanctified, that they may be set apart for this great work which he has given them to do: 'As thou hast sent me into the world, even so have I also sent them into the world. And for their sakes I sanctify myself, that they also might be sanctified through the truth' (v. 19). He sanctifies himself and he wants them to be sanctified in the same way. That throws an interesting light on the meaning of sanctification. If you just extract the word 'sanctify', what our Lord is praying here is that these Christians may have some additional blessing of sanctification. But you can see at once, when you take it in its context, that it again means that he is still concerned about this great and grand objective which he always has in the forefront of his mind and of his heart.

There, then, is a general analysis of his prayer for these people. Why does he pray for them? Well, we have seen the answer. What does he pray for them? Once again we have seen that the requests and petitions arise naturally and inevitably from a consideration of who these people are, the circumstances in which they are placed and the task which they have been given to do. And the only further point I would make here is one which is surely of the greatest possible value, something which comes with comfort and with consolation and encouragement, namely, what we see here in this section about the Lord himself. Here he is praying for his followers, not only for those immediately of his own time but for all who are going to believe in him throughout the centuries, and therefore for us. Let us look at him as he thus prays; let us look at certain things which stand out very clearly about his person. Notice his claims. He says, for instance, 'They ... have known surely that I came out from thee' (v. 8). Here is, apparently, one who is just a man. He is to be taken by cruel people in apparent helplessness and weakness and is to be crucified on a cross, yet he speaks of himself as one who has come out from God. Here is another great assertion of his unique deity: he is proclaiming that he is the eternal Son of

God come from heaven to earth to dwell among men. He repeats it by saying, 'Thou didst send me.' He is not one who has just been born like everybody else, he has been sent by God into this world.

Then in verse 10 he does not hesitate to say a thing like this: 'I am glorified in them' – a tremendous assertion that he is not only man, he is the Son of God, verily God himself, and that as he is the glory of the Father, so the disciples are to be his glory. He has glorified the Father, and he is glorified in them by what they are going to be, and what they are going to do. You notice our calling, you notice that we, as Christians, have the privilege of being men and women in him – that through us the Lord Jesus Christ himself is glorified. It is our conception of the Christian that is wrong. I feel more and more that most of our troubles arise from that fact. We must start by contemplating again what a Christian is, how the New Testament describes him, the place in which he is put, the dignity it ascribes to him – the glory, this special relationship to the Lord and to the Father.

And then he says in his prayer, 'That they may be one, even as we are.' He is one with God. He does not hesitate to assert it and to claim it: 'I and my Father are one' (Jn 10:30). He, a carpenter, one who had not passed through the schools, is one with God, God in flesh on the face of the earth – it is stupendous. In other words, to sum it all up, he has been sent by God into the world for this specific task. He said it in verse 4 when he prayed for himself: 'I have glorified thee on the earth: I have finished the work which thou gavest me to do.' There is the most exalted claim that a person in the flesh has ever made, but at the same time, observe his humility. He, who is the Son of God, does not hesitate to say so and to assert it, but notice the way in which he describes his coming into the world. He has been sent into it by God. Did he come to speak of himself and manifest himself and his own glory? No, he says, 'I have manifested thy name unto the men which thou gavest me out of the world.' That is something which should humble and humiliate us to the very dust as we read these gospels and look at this person who is none other than the only begotten Son of God. Observe his self-abasement;

he does not call attention to himself, he is all along manifesting the glory of his Father. It is God's name, the Father's name, that he is concerned about, and here he reminds his Father of that: 'I have manifested thy name ...'

And then we see how he describes the Christians as his Father's people: 'I have manifested thy name unto the men which thou gavest me out of the world.' He does not say, 'I am going to pray to you about my converts', or 'I am coming to you about the people who believe because of my preaching', or 'because of my miracles', or 'because of what I have done'. No, his view of his people is that they are the Father's people, the Father's children, and they believe on him because they have been given to him by God for that purpose. Was there ever such humility, such self-abasement and self-effacement? He is God, very God, and yet everything belongs to the Father, and the praise and the glory are ascribed to him.

Then you notice that in the eighth verse he goes so far as to say, 'I have given unto them the words which thou gavest me', and we find him constantly repeating that right through the gospel records. It is one of the most amazing things of all, that here we have the Son of God teaching the people, and yet he always emphasizes that nothing he says is of himself. This means that he never uses his own thoughts or words. The Father has given him certain words to speak, and he speaks them.

There is something terrifying about this. If that is true of the preaching of the only begotten Son of God, how much more should it be true of our preaching. The business of a man standing in a pulpit is not to speak his own words but to be biblical. He must expound this word because it is God's word, and he must speak the word that he is enabled to speak by the Holy Spirit. Our Lord was in utter subjection to the Father and everything he did and said was that which was given to him by the Father. So I would beg you again to meditate upon this. Consider this picture and examine yourself in the light of it – see the utter humility of our Lord, his self-abasement, his self-effacement and his complete dependence upon his Father.

Then the other thing, as I have already mentioned, is his supreme concern about the glory of God, which comes out everywhere. In both the first and the second sections this is his one petition: 'Father ... glorify thy Son' – why? – 'that thy Son also may glorify thee.' That is the reason – not himself, but that he may go on to glorify the Father to the end. And here he prays the same thing for these disciples. He says that this is really the only motive for making disciples at all, it is the only reason for preaching the gospel. Let us not misunderstand one another about this, but, I repeat, over and above our concern for the souls of men and their salvation should be our concern for the glory of God. What we should emphasize to men and women outside Christ and sinners in the world today is not, primarily, the fact that they are sinners, and unhappy because they are sinners, but the fact that their sin is an assault upon God and is detracting from his glory. Our concern about the glory of God should come even before our concern for the state and the condition of the sinner. It was true of our Lord, and it is he who sends us out.

But let me end on this note. Observe his care for his followers. He reminds his Father that he kept them while he was in the world. How easy it is to read the gospels without seeing that all the while he is watching them, and keeping them, and shielding them against the enemy. But now he is going out of the world and here he is praying to his Father to keep them. He pleads with him to look after them and commits them to his care. They are his Father's but they have been given to him and he gives them back – 'keep them from the evil' (v. 15). If we but realized the concern of our Saviour for us as we are tried and tempted and beset by sin and Satan, it would revolutionize our whole attitude towards everything.

And, last of all, we should note his loving attitude towards them. Some astounding things are said here. Indeed we would almost be right to query them when we read what he says of these disciples: 'I have manifested thy name unto the men which thou gavest me out of the world' – then notice – 'thine they were, and thou gavest them me; and they have kept thy word.'

How can he say that? As we read the gospels and look at these disciples, we see them quarrelling with one another, we see their jealousy of one another and their desire for pre-eminence over one another, and finally we read how at the end they all forsook him and fled. Yet what he said about them was, 'they have kept thy word'. He did not criticize them, he prayed for them. I thank God for this above everything else. 'If thou, Lord, shouldest mark iniquities, O Lord, who shall stand? But there is forgiveness with thee, that thou mayest be feared' (Ps 130:3–4). We have such a High Priest, sympathetic and understanding, loving, seeing what is true of us, committing us to God in terms like that, not mentioning the deficiencies, the weaknesses, the faults and the failures, but saying, 'they have kept thy word'. And because of that he commends us to God the Father and beseeches his loving protection around and about us.

Well, we have simply entered into the portals. These are but preliminary considerations on our way into this magnificent edifice in which we shall be reminded, as I have been trying to show you, of our Lord's own view of the Christian, what he is, his task, his business in the world, his destiny, and the glory which belongs to him.

May God bless these thoughts to our minds and to our hearts, and, above everything, let us ever think of him, our faithful High Priest, our Representative, our Advocate, our Intercessor, who, in heaven and in glory at this moment, has the same character as he had when he prayed on earth for his followers.

2

Not of the World

I pray for them: I pray not for the world, but for them which thou hast given me; for they are thine (v. 9).

We have seen that before our Lord makes specific requests for his people, he first gives his reasons for praying for them. So in this verse he starts off with a definition and description of the people for whom he is praying, and, therefore, of the Christian. This, then, is his first reason for praying for them and it is this which we must now consider together. The more I try to live this Christian life and the more I read the New Testament, the more convinced I am that the trouble with most of us is that we have never truly realized what it is to be a Christian. It is our whole conception of what a Christian is, and of what the Christian life is meant to be, that is so defective, and that is why we miss so many blessings. That is why, too, we are often so troubled and perplexed and bewildered and why we react as we do to so many of the things that happen to us in this life and in this world. If only we understood what the Christian really is and the position in which he is placed, if only we realized the privilege and the possibilities of that position, and, above everything, the glorious destiny of everyone who is truly a Christian, then our entire outlook would be completely changed. It would be revolutionized, or, as Paul puts it in writing to the Romans, our whole outlook would be transformed by the renewing of our minds (Rom 12:2).

20

The New Testament is literally full of this teaching; there is a sense in which it can be said quite truly that starting with Acts and going right through to the end of Revelation, there is only one theme, and that is the theme of what a Christian is. Why were these New Testament epistles written? It is clear that they were not written merely because the men who wrote them rather liked writing letters! No, there was a reason for every letter, there is a kind of urgency behind every one of them, because the men who wrote the letters were pastors who were concerned about the souls of the people to whom they were writing. The early Christians were in this difficult world, in which you and I still have to live, they were surrounded by very many problems, and all these letters were written in order to help them to live as Christians in such a world. You can sum up the argument of every letter by putting it like this: what all the writers are saying, in effect, is, 'If you only realized who and what you are, you would have gone eighty per cent of the way to being a complete victor over everything that assails you.' Read the introductions, listen to these writers in their salutations; they remind the people of who they are and of what God has done in Christ, and therefore of all the possibilities which are theirs.

That is the whole case, and surely there is nothing that we need more at the present time than just this reminder. That is the way, and the *only* way, according to the New Testament, in which we can live in a world like this, and, furthermore, that is not only the case of the New Testament, it is substantiated and proved in the long history of the Christian church. Read the stories and accounts of every period of revival and reawakening, when the Holy Spirit has been present in power and in might. At such times men and women have known these things as they should be known, and they have been able to rise above all their circumstances. Indeed, you cannot understand the history of the church throughout the centuries apart from this. Think of every revival and period of reformation, all the great history, the stories of the martyrs and confessors, and all that stands out so gloriously in church history – how do you explain it? There is only one explanation: those people knew what it was to be a

Christian. Their view of this was the New Testament view of the Christian and the result was that they could defy tyrants without any fear, they could look into the face of death and say, 'It is well.' They knew who they were, and where they were going. They were not afraid of men, of death, or even of hell, because they knew their position in the Lord Jesus Christ, and the result was that these people triumphed.

We are reminded of this when we read that great eleventh chapter of the Epistle to the Hebrews – indeed it is the whole case of the New Testament, and once we accept this view, then like Abraham, and Moses and all the rest, we can go on 'as seeing him who is invisible' (Heb 11:27). We can go out not knowing where we are going, but quite happily, because we know that he is with us. And in his prayer here our Lord seems to me to start at that very point. He knows that the supreme thing for the disciples, in this world, is that they should be certain of these great centralities. Perhaps I should pause and ask a question at this point. How do you and I react to the things that happen to us in this life, and in this world with all its uncertainty? Now I argue that what determines that, finally, is our view of ourselves as Christians.

We must, therefore, consider what our Lord has to say about the Christian. Our method, you remember, of approaching this paragraph is first of all to extract the doctrine, then, having done that, to go back to the details in the light of that doctrine. Here, then, is the essential doctrine – the character of the Christian – and the first thing I notice is a negative. He says in the first phrase, 'I have manifested thy name unto the men which thou gavest me *out of the world.*' Now that is the theme, that is the first thing he says about the Christian. Need I apologize again for starting with a negative? If I understand the times in which you and I are living, I think that the greatest need is for negatives. People do not like them, they so easily condemn us, but whether we like it or not, the first thing that is true of the Christian is that he is not of this world, and does not belong to it. Now you notice that in this one section he repeats that four times. Verse 6: 'I have manifested thy name unto the men which thou gavest me out of the world'; verse 9: 'I pray for them: I pray not for the world, but for them which thou hast given me'; again, verse 14: 'I have given them thy word; and the world hath hated them, because they are not of the world, even as I am not of the world'; and then verse 16: 'They are not of the world even as I am not of the world'. Our Lord goes on repeating that phrase because he wants to impress it upon us. The first thing that is true about the Christian is that he does not belong to this world.

This is, obviously, a very big point. I chose to quote verse 9 as my particular text here because it seems to put it more pointedly than any of the others. Our Lord says that he prays for them only. He does not pray for the world; there is only one prayer that he offers for the world, and there is only one prayer that we should offer for the world, and that is that it may be saved. But here he is praying and interceding for all who belong to him. He is praying as the mediator, offering a particular prayer as the representative of his own people, and that is where the practical urgency comes in. In this frightening and uncertain world in which we find ourselves, surely, if we are Christian at all, we must feel that the biggest and the most important thing for us to know is whether or not the Lord Jesus Christ is praying and interceding for us.

In the light of this, it is vital that we should ask ourselves the question: am I of the world or am I not? That is the fundamental distinction which runs right through the Bible from beginning to end. Again I refer you to Hebrews 11, and you find the same thing, also, right through the Old Testament. There are only two groups of people in the world today – those who are of the world and those who belong to Christ. In the last analysis there is no other division or distinction that has the slightest importance or relevance. That is why most of us are defeated by life in this world – we recognize other distinctions that are quite unimportant. But when we all come to die, does it make the slightest difference as to which political party we belong to? Does it matter whether we are rich or poor, learned or otherwise? Does it matter what our social status is? It is all utterly irrelevant, it does not matter. As the old English proverb says,

'Death is the grand leveller.'

How foolish we are, how superficial we are, to bother ourselves, as we do, with these other distinctions. I know that, in a
sense, they have their place, but what I am saying here is that
they are not fundamental things. There is only one fundamental
distinction and that is whether we belong to the world or to
Christ. That is the only thing that matters on our death-bed, the
other things will not be of the slightest value to us, they will be
utterly insignificant.

The Christian, then, is one who has been separated from the
world. 'Ah!' says someone, 'There you are, you Christians,
putting yourselves into a separate compartment and category.'
That is quite right – I do not resent that charge at all. I deliberately assert that I am not of the world, I am not in the same
category as those who belong to it and I thank God for that. It is
not something to be ashamed of, but something to glory in.
What a tragedy it is that Christian people seem to be ashamed of
this and are ever trying to conform to the world. We should
desire to be entirely different, to be not of the world as he was
not of it. We are meant to be marked men and women, different
in every respect. This, therefore, is what we must consider
together in order to make quite certain that we can rest in the
quiet confidence and assurance that the Lord Jesus Christ is concerned about us and that he is interceding on our behalf. He
says, you remember, 'Neither pray I for these alone, but for
them also which shall believe on me through their word' – and
that is you and me.

Scripture is full of this doctrine. We have seen Paul's appeal to
the Romans: 'Be not conformed to this world: but be ye transformed by the renewing of your mind' (Rom 12:2). James says
the same thing: 'Know ye not that the friendship of the world is
enmity with God? whosoever therefore will be a friend of the
world is the enemy of God' (Jas 4:4). Could anything be plainer
or clearer than that? Then let me remind you of those forcible
words in 1 John 2:15–17: 'Love not the world, neither the things
that are in the world. If any man love the world, the love of the
Father is not in him. For all that is in the world, the lust of the

flesh, and the lust of the eyes, and the pride of life, is not of the Father, but is of the world. And the world passeth away, and the lust thereof: but he that doeth the will of God abideth for ever.' This is a momentous statement. And we find John saying exactly the same thing in chapter 5 of that same epistle: 'We know we are of God, and the whole world lieth in wickedness', or 'in the evil one' (v. 19).

Obviously, therefore, the practical question for us is to know for certain that we are 'not of the world', and there are many ways in which that question may be answered. Certain specific distinctions are given, and I want just to call your attention to these basic points. Take, for instance, how Paul puts it in Ephesians 2:1-3, 'You hath he quickened, who were dead in trespasses and sins; wherein in time past ye walked according to the course of this world, according to the prince of the power of the air, the spirit that now worketh in the children of disobedience. Among whom also we all had our conversation in times past in the lusts of our flesh, fulfilling the desires of the flesh and of the mind; and were by nature the children of wrath, even as others.' That is a most comprehensive definition of what it means to belong to the world, and so, too, is the statement quoted above from 1 John 2.

So let us face the question in the light of these definitions. To be of the world can be summed up like this – it is life, thought of and lived, apart from God. In other words, what decides definitely and specifically whether you and I are of the world or not is not so much what we may do in particular as our fundamental attitude. It is an attitude towards everything, towards God, towards ourselves, and towards life in this world; in the last analysis, to be of the world is to view all these things apart from God. So let us get rid of the idea that worldliness just means going to the theatre or the cinema; do not think that if you do this or that you are therefore a worldly person. It is not that, for there are many people who never do any of these things but who, according to the Scriptures, are thoroughly worldly-minded. Indeed – and this is a terrible thing – as I understand this definition, you can even subscribe to the Christian faith in an orthodox manner and still be of the world. If anybody disputes this, let me give you my authority at once. The word uttered by our Lord to those people who at the last day shall say, Lord, Lord, haven't we done this, that and the other in your name? is, Depart from me, I never knew you – you do not belong, you never have belonged to me (Mt 25:31–46). To belong to the world is a fundamental attitude, and, as I am going to show you, we betray ourselves and our attitude by what we are in general, and by the way in which that is manifested in various respects.

To be of the world – and this is repeated by the apostles – means that we are governed by the mind and the outlook and the way of this world in which we live. Paul says in Ephesians 2:2 that we are governed by 'the prince of the power of the air, the spirit that now worketh in the children of disobedience'. In 2 Corinthians 4:4 he talks about the 'god of this world' and it is the essence of biblical teaching that this world and its ways are under the dominion of Satan. According to this teaching, everybody who is of the world is governed and guided and dominated and controlled by that outlook which is opposed to God. Consequently, every man who is not a Christian and who talks so much about his free will is the greatest dupe of all. He is so much a slave of Satan that he does not know it; he is so blind that he cannot even begin to think about it. It is a domination, which holds us in its grip, and of course we all know about it from experience. The greatest tyranny which we have to meet in this life is that of the worldly outlook. It insinuates itself into our thinking everywhere, and we get it immediately we are born. We belong to a particular family and have certain ideas before we are very old; we turn to our newspapers and they are always suggesting things, as do the books we read. Indeed, everything seems to be suggesting a way of life to us, and we absorb it unconsciously – it is a domination, it is 'the god of this world'. And the first thing that happens to a man when he is convicted of sin and begins to repent is that he realizes the thraldom of the world and its way.

But let me divide it up into detail in order that we may think it through at our leisure. The world tends to control our thought, our outlook, and our mentality. The fact of the matter is that the whole thinking of the world conforms to a pattern. Oh, I know all about the different schools of thought, but in the end they all conform to a pattern, and they all have something in common. But surely, says someone, there is nothing in common between the communist and the man who is extreme on the other side? I say that there is; they are both very much interested in material things and material welfare and they are both probably controlled by this. There is a fundamental, common platform and they only differ in detail. One man says, 'I ought to have this', and the other man says, 'No, I ought to have it' and they quarrel with each other, but there is really no quarrel in their thought and outlook – 'One touch of nature makes the whole world kin.'

The fundamental philosophy common to all is that all this thinking is entirely confined to this world. It is on that level and never rises above it. It has no revelation, it does not believe in such a thing – and indeed that is another way of dividing everybody in the world today. The Christian's fundamental thinking is controlled by the Bible, by revelation from above. Philosophy – what man thinks, what man has discovered – that is the characteristic of the world, and it is at that point that you see the utter folly of all the other divisions, because worldly thinking is all on the human level, and it never contains anything from above. It is an outlook which never thinks of anything beyond this world, and this is true in all the different realms and departments. There is a hatred of the thought of death in the world today. I do not care which group of society people may come from, or what kind of person they are. They all hate it because they are living entirely for this life and for this world, and they are not prepared to consider anything beyond it. That is characteristic of the worldly outlook.

But I can sum it all up by saying that the man who belongs to the world is completely dead to spiritual things. The classic statement of this is again made by the apostle Paul. These things, he says, are spiritual, and 'the natural man receiveth not the things of the Spirit of God: for they are foolishness unto him: neither can he know them, because they are spiritually discerned' (1 Cor 2:14). 'You hath he quickened,' he says in another passage, 'who were dead in trespasses and sins' (Eph 2:1) – dead to everything that is of the Spirit and of the soul and of eternity. These things make no impact upon those who are in the world. They do not see anything in them and they cannot understand people wasting their time on these things, which they find so dull. These poor people are just confessing that they are spiritually dead in trespasses and in sins and their souls are in a state of death.

But obviously this also manifests itself in the desires and pleasures, and the ambitions of such people. The general description is 'the lust of the flesh, and the lust of the eyes and the pride of life' (1 Jn 2:16), and that is a perfect analysis. In some people it seems to be a delight in the things that belong to the animal, to nature, to pure carnality. Life is full of it today, and men and women are only living to the flesh. They must always be reading about it, so the newspapers and the periodicals are full of it. That is life, they say – it is astounding, but how true it is – the lust of the flesh.

Then the lust of the eye. This is a little more refined, not quite so gross, but it is the same thing. It is a concern about personal appearance. Think of the space that is given to this, too, in the press; think of the appalling amount of time and thought and money which people give merely to how they look, or to the figure they cut. They even study and practise the very way they walk – a living soul and spirit, made in the image of God! – but that is the world.

And then the pride of life, which is even more subtle than the lust of the eye. The things we boast of, the things about which we are so proud: our birth, our family, our background, our forebears, the school we went to, the university in which we studied – are not these the things that are the pride of life? We preen and pride ourselves on something that we are, and that somebody else is not. But it is all entirely of the flesh and the animal. These things are utterly irrelevant before God but they are the things that the world likes – the pride of life, intellectual pride. These are the things that are characteristic of the world, this is where it derives its pleasure, this is its ambition. It is exalted by these things, it lives for them, it talks about them. These are the things which are supreme in people's lives, this is their whole outlook, and, I ask a solemn question, can it be said that those of us who are in the realm of the church are free from such things? Let every man examine himself.

And, finally, the world shows itself in conduct, the conduct which corresponds with the outlook and the desire. The result is that people who are in the world live only for such things and on such a level. Let me put it quite plainly, for I want to show how universal this is. It is in all of us until the grace of God comes into our life and shows what it is, and makes us heed it, and delivers us out of it. It is a terrible thing to think that there are many people around us who are living this sort of life. They are not guilty of the things I have just been mentioning but they are just living life for themselves and their families. Think of many quite ordinary people, quite respectable people. They are not concerned about these subtle forms of sin which I have been enumerating, but the tragedy about them is that they are just living for their own little family circle. They never think of God and they never praise him. There are many thousands of such families living within the confines of life and time on earth, never rising above it all.

All that, then, is the negative, it is 'of the world'. That, says our Lord, is the kind of life which such people lead and they are not the ones I am praying for here.

But now let us look at the positive. The Christian is not like that, the Christian is like Christ himself: 'I have manifested thy name unto the men which thou gavest me out of the world: thine they were, and thou gavest them me, and they have kept thy word.' And again in verse 16: 'They are not of the world, even as I am not of the world.' Do I want to know for certain whether I am a Christian? Well, am I like those who are of the world? If I am not, I can take comfort, but I must be positive also. I must be like the Lord Jesus Christ. He says his people are like him. Is he the centre of my life? Is my relationship to God the controlling thing in my life? I am not saying I am perfect, but, as I understand this teaching, I do say that I cannot be a

Christian unless I can say quite honestly that the basis of my life
is in God and that he is at the centre. However much I may fail
from time to time in practice, I am centred on God. This means,
therefore, that in terms of the revelation of the Bible, I, like
those people in Hebrews 11, view all things in this life and world
according to that outlook. My governing thought is that I am a
pilgrim and a stranger in this world, going on to God, so that of
necessity I spend my time in thinking of my soul and of my
destiny. I do not get annoyed when somebody faces me with the
fact of death, because I remind myself of it day by day; I realize
that this is the one thing I have to start with and that I am a fool
if I do not. The Christian always holds that before him, his
whole life is lived under God and he realizes the nature of life in
this world. He is controlling his life so that he does not foolishly
spend most of his time and energy in trying to forget that it must
come to an end. He deliberately keeps that before him.

And from that, of course, follows this desire to know God and
his love in Christ; a desire to be more like Christ; a desire to be
holy; a desire to spend more and more time in fellowship with
God and with Christ, that we may conform more and more to
his image; a desire to be well pleasing in God's sight. Let me put it
as strongly as I can. When a man is like Christ he hates the world
– the outlook, not the people – the mentality, the type of life. He
realizes it is subtle, in that it is trying to keep him from God,
whatever form it may take. He realizes, too, that these things are
damnable, and against God. They take a pride in something that
belongs to a fallen world, and he hates it as Christ hated it. He
turns his back upon it, so he prays a great deal to be delivered
from it. He separates himself as much as he can to meditate upon
heavenly things and he lives his life in the fear of God.

That is what the Bible tells us is meant by not being of the
world even as Christ was not of the world (v.16). Oh my
beloved friends, let me plead with you to face this, to face it
every day and never to forget it. The consequences are so vital.
If you and I are of the world it means that Christ is not praying
for us, but if we do belong to him we are not of the world.
Remember that God is your Father and that he will not let any-

thing happen to you that will harm you. That does not mean that no distressing event will befall you, but that when it does, in the amazing will and purpose of God, even that is going to be a good thing, and you will understand it in glory. What a wonderful thing it is to go through life knowing that your life is in the hands of God, knowing that your Father is thus concerned about you and that your blessed Mediator who prayed for you on earth is still interceding for you in heaven.

To be 'not of the world' means that we are children of God, though once we were 'children of wrath'. Let us make no mistake about this. If you and I go out of this life belonging to the world, and of the world, we have nothing to look forward to but wrath. I do not know if you can tell me of a sadder statement in Scripture than John 17:9: 'I pray not for the world.' Those who are of the world are under the wrath of God until they come out of that position, until they believe in Christ and until they are saved and reconciled to God. He does not pray for them, they are just left, and it is an appalling thing to think that people who go out like that go to nothing but the wrath of God. Oh the folly of being of the world! For, as John tells us, the world passes away and the lust thereof. Is it not astounding that everybody does not realize that? Let us pay heed to the warning of things that happen. The world is passing away. Your pride in your appearance, in your life and position, all you have and what you are, my friend, is decaying and rotting even as you are boasting of it. And a day will come when it will be useless and your naked soul will be there alone. 'The world passeth away, and the lust thereof: but he that doeth the will of God abideth for ever' (1 Jn 2:17).

I trust that as the result of this examination we are all able to say quietly and to the glory of God, 'I am not of the world, I belong to God in Jesus Christ and I am safe in his holy, heavenly keeping. Come what may, I can say that "neither death, nor life, nor angels, nor principalities, nor powers, nor things present, nor things to come, nor height, nor depth, nor any other creature, shall be able to separate us from the love of God, which is in Christ Jesus our Lord".'

3

God's People

I have manifested thy name unto the men which thou gavest me out of the world: thine they were, and thou gavest them me; and they have kept thy word (v.6).

In our last study we saw that nothing is more important and reassuring in a world like this than to be sure that the Lord Jesus Christ is praying for us and interceding on our behalf. But now we must go on to the next step. We have seen that Christians are people who are not of the world. There is a great division in mankind: there are those who belong to the world and those who do not. The second group have been placed in a special position. They have been segregated from everybody else, and the great question that arises at once is what has happened to them and why? Why should they be the special object of our Lord's solicitude and care? Why this fundamental division in mankind? What is it about Christian people that puts them into a separate position?

That is one of the most profound and fundamental questions that a human being can ever consider. The fact is beyond dispute, as we saw in our last study, but let me put it still more directly. As we think of the great mass of people in the world today who are leading worldly lives, what is it that makes us different? Why are we not like them? In saying that, I am not speaking like a Pharisee, for as I have already pointed out, a Christian must know that he is different. If he does not know that, then he is not a Christian at all, because the term itself describes certain people. It is not that the Christian says in a superior way, 'I thank God that I am not like that other man.' We shall see, however, that we do use those same words, not as the Pharisee used them but in a very different manner.

Why, then, are Christian people not of the world? It is because *they are God's people.* 'I have manifested thy name' – to whom? – 'unto the men which thou gavest me out of the world: thine they were, and thou gavest them me.' That is the answer. That is the first, and indeed the ultimate explanation, the one which includes all the others. We hope later to show how exactly this was done, and how we are put into that position, but the fundamental answer to the question is that we are there and that we are what we are because we are God's people.

Here we come again to one of those foundational doctrines of the Bible and of the Christian faith and it is one of the most glorious of all the doctrines. It is a point which is constantly neglected in our day, and we neglect it to the great impoverishment of our souls and Christian experience. This is something which is central to the whole biblical view of life, and especially of salvation. The importance of the doctrine can be seen at a glance in this very chapter. Whenever our Lord repeats a thing we can be quite sure that he regards it as absolutely vital. We are familiar with the fact that whenever he introduces a statement by saying, 'Verily, verily' we ought to pay unusual attention to it, so, if he repeats a statement frequently in a short space, we can be equally certain that it is something which we should lay hold of very firmly. Now you notice how he repeats it in this particular section. Here it is in verse 6, but again we have it in verse 9: 'I pray for them: I pray not for the world, but for them which thou hast given me; for they are thine.' In verse 10 he says, 'All mine are thine, and thine are mine; and I am glorified in them', and then again in verse 11: 'And now I am no more in the world, but these are in the world, and I come to thee. Holy Father, keep through thine own name those whom thou hast given me, that they may be one, as we are one.' Finally, in verse 12 he says, 'While I was with them in the world, I kept them in thy name: those that thou

gavest me I have kept, and none of them is lost, but the son of
perdition; that the scripture might be fulfilled.'

So we have this statement five times in this passage, and we
have already met it in verse 2 of the first section: 'As thou hast
given him power over all flesh, that he should give eternal life
to as many as thou hast given him.' And we will find it again in
the last section, in verse 24: 'Father, I will that they also, whom
thou hast given me, be with me where I am; that they may
behold my glory, which thou hast given me.' Thus, in the space
of these twenty-six verses, our Lord makes that particular statement seven times. In this short prayer he seven times describes
the people for whom he is praying, his followers, as those who
have been given to him by God.

Nothing, then, ought to establish in our minds the all-impor-
tance of this doctrine and teaching more than that, but you will
also find that it is something which is taught everywhere in the
New Testament. We find it in John 6:37 where our Lord says,
'All that the Father giveth me shall come to me; and him that
cometh to me I will in no wise cast out'; and again in verse 39
where he says that he will keep all that the Father has given to
him and that he will raise them up at the last day. It is exactly
the same principle: the ones who will come to him are the ones
whom the Father has given him. And further on in chapter 6,
in verse 44, we read, 'No man cometh to me' – he puts it in a
slightly different way – 'except the Father ... draw him.' This
teaching is given in a very remarkable manner in that sixth chapter of John's gospel, but indeed, as I said, it is a doctrine which
is taught everywhere throughout the New Testament.

It is found, for instance, throughout that mighty first chapter
of the Epistle to the Ephesians, but especially in Paul's prayer for
the church at Ephesus. He prays that the eyes of their understanding may be enlightened. He wants them to grasp this truth with
their minds and with their understanding because it is so vital. He
prays that they may know what is the hope of their calling and
then, secondly, what is 'the riches of the glory of his inheritance'
– God's inheritance – 'in the saints', which just means this very
matter that we are looking at together. I want you to know, he

says, and to see yourselves, as God's inheritance. I want you to
grasp this great idea of God's special segregated people. It is his
prayer, above everything else, that these people might know this.

Consider, too, what he wrote to Timothy. Timothy was
very troubled and worried about certain things that were happening in some of the churches for which he was responsible,
and Paul, in effect, says, 'Timothy, you need not be troubled,
"The Lord knoweth them that are his."' He knows his own
people and that means that he not only knows them but he looks
after them, he keeps his eye upon them. Then in Hebrews 2:13
these words are applied to our Lord: 'Behold I and the children
which God hath given me.' That is how the Lord Jesus Christ
refers to Christians and to the members of his church. Peter also
writes on the same theme in his epistle: 'Ye are a chosen generation, a royal priesthood, an holy nation, a peculiar people' (1 Pet
2:9), which means, a people for God's special interest and possession. I could go on and give you other quotations from the
New Testament, but look them up for yourselves, and you will
find that it is a doctrine which keeps on appearing everywhere.

Of course you have it equally strikingly in the Old Testament. Nothing perhaps is more true of the Old Testament than
to say that it is, in a sense, just an elaboration of this idea of God's
people, God's peculiar interest in his own people, the Children
of Israel, and his dealings with them. All the nations of the
world belong to God, but these are his special people, the people
of his choice. For instance, those words which I have just quoted
from Peter's epistle were first of all applied in Exodus 19 to the
Children of Israel, just before the giving of the Law when God
reminded them that they were his own special people. Indeed, I
do not hesitate to assert that we do not understand the Bible in a
radical sense unless we grasp this doctrine of God's people. Paul
sums it up in Romans 11 by talking about the 'fulness of the
Gentiles': '… until the fulness of the Gentiles be come in. And so
all Israel shall be saved' (vv 25–26) that is, God's people, Israel,
and all God's special people throughout the ages.

This teaching, therefore, is vital and because of that, because
of its prominence in the Scriptures, quite apart from the conso-

lation it gives to us, we must look at it a little more closely. What does it mean? I would suggest to you that it means something like this: God has chosen and marked out and separated a people for himself. There is no question about that. We have seen that it is the biblical teaching from beginning to end. God has put these people there on one side, on their own, in a special position of privilege and of blessing. 'Thine they were, and thou gavest them me.' It is ultimately the action of God himself.

Take the argument in Ephesians 1, in which such mighty terms are used. Let me plead with you, when you read a great chapter like that, to forget prejudice and not be so foolish that you stop at certain words in a way which raises the old arguments and enters at once into some ridiculous attempt to understand the mind of the eternal God. It is tragic that we should rob ourselves of these great doctrines and their benefits, and indeed that we should insult God himself and his gracious purpose, by taking up our little positions. Let us read a wonderful chapter like this and just listen to what it says. It tells us that God has done this before the foundation of the world, that before you and I were ever born, before the world was ever created, we were then known to God. He himself has determined these things. When you pause to think about it, it is one of the most staggering things that can ever come to a man's mind and comprehension, that though man sinned and rebelled, and as a result brought chaos into the universe, this almighty God who made the world and created everything in it, should nevertheless be concerned in this way and should separate certain people unto himself.

Secondly, he has done this solely and entirely of his own grace and love and not because of anything that he saw or found or ever will find in us. He has done this moved by nothing but his own glorious, ineffable nature and character. Oh, I do not understand it, I do not understand it from any aspect, and it is when we begin to try to understand these things that we always get into trouble. Many questions are thrown up at us; for example, 'Why did he only choose certain people and not others?' Or, to put it the other way round, 'If my brothers were not cho-

sen, why did he ever choose me?' I do not understand it either
way, and one is as baffling as the other. But let us leave our
pigmy understanding to the realm of time and earth, and let us
look at the glorious statement, which is that in spite of the fact
that we are all born in sin and 'shapen in iniquity' (Ps 51:5), in
spite of the fact that we are all by nature the children of wrath,
though we all by nature hate God and deliberately disobey him
and follow our own desires and our own lusts and self-will, and
glory in ourselves rather than in him, in spite of the arrogance
and pride and rebellion of all men, in spite of all these things, this
almighty God has looked upon certain people and has placed his
mark upon them. And not only that. He has done something to
them and about them, and has taken them from that evil world
into which they were born and has set them aside as his own special people.

Then we come to the next step, which is that he desires us as
his own particular possession and portion, and ultimately as
those who are to share his glory. Look again at Paul's prayer for
the Ephesian church in Ephesians 1. It is that they may know
what is 'the hope of his calling, and what the riches of the glory
of his inheritance in the saints'. To talk about God's inheritance
in the saints, the God who made everything and to whom all
things belong, and by whom all things are, to talk in this way is
the most amazing and daring piece of anthropomorphism that
Paul ever produced, and yet he has to put it like that in order to
give them an understanding of it. What he means is that these
are the people in whom God delights and this is what God is
going to enjoy.

Let me give an illustration in order to make this point clear – I
think we are entitled to do so in terms of the apostle's language.
Take a child who has many toys and dolls, all of which he likes.
Yes, but there is one particular favourite, the doll which is
always with him and sleeps with him . The child is fond of them
all but that one is something special. And it is the same with us.
We all have certain possessions which we prefer to others, there
is always something especially dear and of concern and interest
to us. That is the idea – that the great Lord of the universe has a

special object of interest and affection in his own people, in those whom he has taken and, as Paul puts it in writing to the Galatians, separated out of this evil world and put into a special category and compartment. That is the whole message of the Bible – God preparing for himself a people who are going to be his joy and rejoicing throughout eternity. So that is the beginning of the great truth. A Christian is one who is not of the world because God has chosen him – it all starts with the heart of the Eternal himself.

But let me take it a step further. God who had thus separated and marked a people for himself, then gave them to Christ: 'I have manifested thy name unto the men which thou gavest me out of the world'; 'As thou hast given him power over all flesh, that he should give eternal life to as many as thou hast given him.' It is always that. This is not merely a manifestation of our Lord's astounding humility, it is a literal, actual fact. Let us look at it like this. As we saw in our study of the first section of this prayer, a covenant was made between the Father and the Son; that is what the Bible tells us, and that is why I thank God for it – that we can enter into such glorious depths and swim in such oceans of mighty thought. This covenant was to the effect that the Father handed over these people whom he had chosen for himself before the foundation of the world. He handed them to the Son in order that the Son might make of them a people fit for God's special possession and enjoyment. So when the Son left heaven to come on earth, to be born as a babe in Bethlehem and to do all that he did, he was coming to carry out that plan. He came because God had handed these people to him and the Father had said, in effect, 'These people cannot be my people as they are. I have chosen them but they are not yet fit and I cannot truly enjoy them until they are. So I give them to you. Go and save them, go and redeem them, go and sanctify them and make them a people that I can enjoy and in whom I shall have my great joy and pleasure.'

So the Lord Jesus Christ came from heaven to earth in order to do that. That is the whole meaning of the incarnation, of his suffering, and of his being subjected to temptation. It is the whole meaning of his agony in the Garden, his death upon the cross, his resurrection and of everything else that he did. It has all been done for these people of God. The design is to prepare them for the Father in order to make them fit and meet for him. So as we look at the accounts in the gospels and see all that happened to our blessed Lord, we just realize that all that was done for us, for these people amongst whom we find ourselves, as the result of God's grace. Our Lord is described as the Mediator of the New Covenant; God made a covenant with him. Our Lord took those whom God had given him and he prepared them for God because they are God's peculiar possession.

And the end will be this, according to 1 Corinthians 15:24–25: 'Then cometh the end, when he shall have delivered up the kingdom to God, even the Father; when he shall have put down all rule and all authority and power. For he must reign, till he hath put all enemies under his feet.' When the last enemy shall have been destroyed, when every vestige of sin and evil shall be removed and purged out of the whole cosmos, when the contract has been finally completed, our Lord will have perfected the people and he will hand them back. The kingdom will be handed back to the Father and God shall be all and in all. That is what this teaching about God's people really means, and that is what it involves.

Let me, finally, draw certain simple, obvious conclusions from this high and exalted doctrine. As I look at these things and meditate upon them, my first conclusion is that our normal, ordinary view of salvation is hopelessly and ridiculously inadequate. Our trouble is that we always start with ourselves instead of starting with God. Instead of going to the Bible and looking at its revelation and discovering there what salvation means, I start with myself and certain things that I want and desire, certain benefits that I always want to enjoy in this life and in this world. I want forgiveness of sins; I want peace of conscience and of mind; I want enjoyment and happiness; I want to be delivered from certain sins; I want guidance; I want this and that; and my whole conception of salvation is reduced to that level.

Do not misunderstand me, the Christian salvation does those

things and contains them all, but how pathetic it is that we should start in that way and only look at that. How sad that we should not look at it in this other way and start with God – before the foundation of the world – and see this great and gracious purpose, and view ourselves as a people brought into it. We do not start with ourselves, but with God and the amazing fact that he should have brought us in and made us to be like this. To me the most wonderful thing of all is not that my sins have been forgiven, nor that I may enjoy certain experiences and blessings as a Christian. The thing that should astound me now and that will astound me to all eternity, especially when I get to heaven and glory and really begin to see it truly, is that I am a child of God, one of God's people.

The psalmist had some insight into this when he said in that graphic phrase of his, 'I had rather be a doorkeeper in the house of my God, than to dwell in the tents of wickedness' (Ps 84:10). He preferred to be in the vestibule, in the portal, of the house of God than to dwell in the greatest palace of the ungodly – it is the relationship that matters. I would sooner be a slave in God's house than be a dictator in the world. Moses chose 'rather to suffer affliction with the people of God, than to enjoy the pleasures of sin for a season' (Heb 11:25). He did so because he was interested in the recompense of the reward, and he did not take a short view. Moses said to himself, in effect, 'This is the overwhelming thing: that I am one of God's people. I do not care what I am now, even though I am only a shepherd away on the far side of a mountain with just a little flock. This is better, because I am God's, than to be accounted great as the son of Pharaoh's daughter.' Once more, it is the relationship that matters, and it seems to me that the tragedy is that we do not know enough about this relationship. Let us forget our particular blessings and enjoyments and realize that we are children of God, we are among God's people, the people whom he knew before the foundation of the world.

The second conclusion that I would draw is that we are very guilty of misunderstanding the work of Jesus Christ. I have two points here. Does it come as a surprise to anybody that, according to this doctrine, it is no part of the work of the Lord Jesus Christ to make us God's people? Have we not always thought that that was his work – that he suffered for us and made us the people of God? But he did not; we were the people of God first and it was God who gave us to him. If that comes as a surprise to us, it is because we read our Bible with prejudiced eyes instead of looking at what it really says. 'Thine they were, and thou gavest them me.'

My second point is equally important. This is that it is no part of the work of the Lord Jesus Christ to secure God's love for us. I am very fond of our hymns, but I always try to remember that they are not divinely inspired, indeed some of them are tragically wrong and misleading. So many of them give the impression that our Lord is having to plead with his Father on our behalf, that God, as it were, is opposed to us, that our Lord has to engage his love for us and secure it for us. This doctrine shows us that it is not a part of the purpose of the Lord Jesus Christ to do that. It is because God loved us that he ever gave us to Christ. Christ has died for us not to secure the love of God for us, but because God has marked out his people before the foundation of the world. He hands them to the Son and says, Go and save them, they are mine, I leave them to you, make them fit for me. For, 'God so loved the world, that he gave his only begotten Son' (Jn 3:16); 'God was in Christ, reconciling the world unto himself' (2 Cor 5:19) – not himself to the world. Oh how foolish we are and what an injustice we do to the name of our God and to his glorious love and grace! How frequently, because we neglect this fundamental doctrine, do we go wrong in our doctrine of the work of the Lord Jesus Christ!

But there are other conclusions which we can draw. Think, in the light of all that I have been saying, of the place we occupy in the interest and love of the Father and the Son. I confess that I am almost overwhelmed when I think of this. I so often spend my time, as I am sure many of you do, wondering why it is that I do not experience more of the love of God; why God does not, as it were, love me more and do things for me. What a terrible thing that is! The trouble is that I do not realize his love to me, that is my difficulty. People often come and say, 'I feel my love for God is so small' – quite right, I say the same thing myself:

> Lord it is my chief complaint,
> That my love is weak and faint.
> *W. Cowper*

That is true, but the best cure is not to try to do things within yourself and work up some love from the depths of your being. The way to love God is to begin to know God's love to you, and this doctrine is the high road to that love. Before time, before the creation of the world, he set his eye upon you, he set his affection upon you, you were marked, you were already put among his people. And all that has been done, all the person and the work of Christ, all this manifestation of his ineffable love, was done because of God's love to you. Therefore, realize his interest in you. The God who has loved you to the extent of sending his only begotten Son to endure and to suffer all that for you, loves you with a love which you will never understand, a love which passes knowledge. If we but knew God's love to us, it would revolutionize our lives.

And then the next conclusion is this: what sort of people ought we to be in the light of all this? Again, we are too troubled about the details of this question of holiness and sanctification – what method must I adopt? What must I do? We have been given lectures and addresses on the mechanism of obtaining this gift or that particular something. I do not see it like that in Scripture. There, I see it put like this – realize who you are. 'Ye shall be holy' – why? – 'for I am holy' (Lev 11:44). You are God's child, and one of his people. The way of holiness is to realize who you are, and always to remember it and the honour of the family, the honour of your Father, the honour of God. 'Every man that hath this hope in him purifieth himself, even as he is pure' (1 Jn 3:3). That is the argument and if you and I but realized our relationship to God now, and the presence of God with us always, it would very soon solve the problem of holiness and sanctification for us. We would not have to be waiting for particular experiences, we would realize that we are one with God and that we are in that relationship, and because of that, everything else is unthinkable.

And ultimately there is our wonderful security. Our Lord says in John 10:28, 'I give unto them eternal life; and they shall never perish, neither shall any man pluck them out of my hand' – we will come to that later. And here he is saying, I have kept them and now that I am going out of the world I hand them back, as it were, to you. Oh the eternal security of all who are God's people and who are known unto him before the foundation of the world!

Beloved friends, let us meditate upon these things; let us not start with self and its little needs, but let us rather lift up our minds and our hearts and contemplate this glorious plan of God into which we have been brought, which we can enjoy, and which is preparing us for that everlasting and eternal glory. Let us pray for ourselves what Paul prayed for the church at Ephesus, that the eyes of our understanding may be opened and that we may know the riches of the glory of his inheritance in us.

4

The Name of God

I have manifested thy name unto the men which thou gavest me out of the world: thine they were, and thou gavest them me; and they have kept thy word. Now they have known that all things what-soever thou hast given me are of thee. For I have given unto them the words which thou gavest me; and they have received them, and have known surely that I came out from thee, and they have believed that thou didst send me (vv. 6–8).

We saw in our last study that God separated us unto himself, and that having done that, he gave us to his Son, who came and worked out redemption for us, to fit us in a full sense to become God's people. The next step, therefore, that we must be concerned about is this: if I am a Christian at all, it is because God has looked upon me and set his mark upon me before I was ever born, before the world was created, but I still want to know how that becomes actual and how it literally becomes operative in me, in my life and in my experience. And that question is answered in these three verses that we are looking at now. To put it another way, what proof have we that this has taken place in us? How do we know that we are Christians? What exactly has happened to us to take us from the world into which we were born? We are all born the children of wrath and enemies of God. We are all born belonging to the world and subject to the prince of the power of the air, 'the spirit that now worketh in the children of disobedience'. We were all there once, says

Paul, and it is true of all of us. So, then, we ask, what has brought us here? And the answer is in the teaching of these three verses. In these verses we are told what it is that makes one a Christian, we are told exactly how it is that one becomes a Christian. There is a most extraordinary definition of the Christian here; everything that is vital will be found in these verses and therefore we must look at them carefully together.

You notice first that the key to understanding the whole passage is that it all depends upon the Lord Jesus Christ himself, he is absolutely central and vital to this matter. Verses 6–8 are all about him and he says the same thing again towards the end of the prayer, in these words: 'O righteous Father, the world hath not known thee: but I have known thee, and these have known that thou hast sent me.' So once more we see that he is at the centre. He himself constantly repeats this, and, too, it is something that is emphasized everywhere in the Scriptures.

Let me put it another way: there is no real knowledge of God except that which comes through the Lord Jesus Christ; as he said, 'I am the way, the truth and the life: no man cometh unto the Father, but by me' (Jn 14:6). No man can really know God without having life eternal. But what is life eternal? He has already told us: 'This is life eternal, that they might know thee the only true God, and Jesus Christ, whom thou hast sent.' We should observe how our Lord goes on repeating this. He puts himself, as it were, in the centre, and says that he is essential; he emphasizes it, and the reason for this is that mankind always thinks that it can arrive at a knowledge of God apart from him. Let me repeat once more that never was this emphasis more essential than it is at this present moment. Constantly and increasingly we find people teaching and saying that God can be known and that certain blessings can be obtained from him, but they never even refer to the name of the Lord Jesus Christ. They hold that you can get some important blessing, like healing, but Christ is not even mentioned. It comes, they claim, from God immediately and directly. But according to the teaching of the Bible there is no true and real knowledge of God except in and through Christ. That is the essential principle of Christianity, it is the meaning of the very term.

How, therefore, does our Lord bring us this knowledge? How does he let us know that we are God's people and that these various and glorious blessings which God is offering his people will become our portion and lot in this world? He answers this question immediately at the beginning of verse 6: 'I have manifested thy name unto the men which thou gavest me out of the world.' Now this is very important. Why does he put it in that way, instead of simply saying, 'I have manifested thee', or, 'I have manifested certain truths to them'? Why does he put it in terms of manifesting the name of God?

The answer is that this is the form in which the Bible habitually puts this particular teaching. In Scripture the name always stands for the character; it stands for the perfection of the person, and for his attributes; it represents what a person really is. The name is that which truly reveals the person and it is the connotation of everything that the person is in essence. Of course we are familiar with that usage of the term. We say about a doctor, for example, that he has 'a very good name'. We mean by this that he has the reputation of being a very good doctor, but we do not put it like that. We say that he has a very good name, and that expression stands for all the propensities and powers, all the skill and all the understanding, that this man happens to have.

Let me remind you of some of the ways in which this word is thus used in the Scriptures. Take, for instance, the story in Genesis 32:22–32 of Jacob at Penuel. It was a momentous night for him. He knew he had to meet his brother Esau the next day and he wondered what was going to happen. It was the most critical moment that Jacob had ever passed through. Having sent forward his goods and possessions and, last of all, his wives and children, Jacob was left alone, and it was then that a man came and began to struggle with him. Jacob realized that this was no ordinary encounter but that it was something divine and supernatural, so as he went on struggling with the man, he summed up all the knowledge that he had and said to him, 'What is thy name?' – I want to possess you, as it were. He knew that the name would tell him everything.

Then, again, the wise man, Solomon, says in one of his proverbs, 'The name of the Lord is a strong tower: the righteous runneth into it, and is safe' (Prov 18:10). In this world with its problems and difficulties and perplexities, there is only one place of safety says this man; it is the name of the Lord. It is like a strong tower and when I am besieged and attacked I run into that tower, and I am surrounded by the name of the Lord, which means everything that God really is, everything that is represented by the name.

Again, we find it in a still more specific form when God appeared to Moses and gave him his great commission and promise. He said to him, 'I appeared unto Abraham, unto Isaac, and unto Jacob, by the name of God Almighty, but by my name Jehovah was I not known to them' (Exod 6:3). In effect, God came to Moses and said, 'I am going to start something new. I am going to do something fresh. There is going to be a great turn-about in the history of my people. From this moment I am going to give you a great assurance, and before anything happens at all, I am going to give you a new name and I want you to realize what is meant by this name.'

We also have a definition of it in Exodus 34: 'The Lord descended in the cloud, and stood with him there, and proclaimed the name of the Lord' (v. 5) and then in verses 6–7 he began to tell Moses certain extraordinary and remarkable things about himself.

So when our Lord here turns to the Father and says, 'I have manifested thy name ...' what he is saying, in effect, is this: 'You sent me into the world in order to manifest and declare your name, and I have done it.' He has done that which was prophesied of him in Psalm 22:22: 'I will declare thy name unto my brethren: in the midst of the congregation will I praise thee.'

Now I want to put this in a very practical form. I wonder whether we have come to realize that the greatest need of everyone in this world is to know the name of God, because, when we know his name, we really know God himself, and are coming into an intimate knowledge of him. The final trouble with all of us is our ignorance of God. We talk about God, we say we pray to him, but the question asked everywhere in the Bible is: do you *know* him? Has he revealed his name to you? Do you know him in the sense that his name is to you a strong tower, and that whatever happens in this world you are absolutely safe because you run into that tower? Have you found the name of the Lord a shield, a protection, a hiding place when everything else has failed, when the world and its wisdom and science and knowledge can do nothing for you, and when your nearest and dearest are standing by looking helplessly on? Do you view things differently because the name of the Lord is there, and because inside the strong tower you are calm and quiet and serene, and full of joy and happiness? Does the name of the Lord protect you against everything? It is meant to do that.

As you read the lives of the saints in the Old Testament, you will find that this was always their lot and their experience. They were always safe and happy: 'When my father and my mother forsake me, then the Lord will take me up' (Ps 27:10). He never fails, but alas, the tragedy with us is that we do not know the Lord in this way. We often feel that he is against us or that he is unjust or unfair to us. People often suggest that he is cruel and unkind. The simple trouble with all such people is that they do not know him, for if they had known him – known his name – they would never harbour such thoughts concerning him. Such people are, of course, entirely without excuse, because God has revealed himself and his name to us. Indeed, even before his Son ever came into this world, God had revealed and manifested his name to the Children of Israel, so that we are altogether without excuse.

Let me, then, remind you of some of the names that God has given and has revealed about himself, and concerning himself even as we find them in the Old Testament. The first term for God that we find appears in a family of names: 'El, 'Elohim, 'El Shaddai, 'El Elyon – the strong and the mighty One. And this is the first thing we always need to know about God. We need to realize his might and strength and power. We talk so glibly about him, we argue and discuss these matters about God and we say what we think he ought to do. But we should remember that we are speaking about the Almighty, the Strong One. There is no limit to his power, he is the Creator, the Originator, of everything, the one who sustains everything – without him nothing can continue to exist at all. The first name of God is a name of strength, of absolute power, of almightiness.

But of course the name to which we must give particular attention is the special name which he revealed to Moses. This name was known before, but now it was given as a name representing certain things – the great name *Jehovah*. When God gave the promise of deliverance to Moses, he said, I am giving you my special name, Jehovah – that is, the self-existent one, the self-subsistant one, he that *is* – 'I am that I am' (Ex 3:14). God tells us that about himself, that he always was – there is no beginning to God. But it is agreed by all that in that self-same name, Jehovah, there is a further suggestion. It is a name that at one and the same time tells us that God is the self-existent one from eternity to eternity and yet at the same time he also becomes something – he becomes known.

In other words, the name Jehovah suggests a continuous and increasing revelation of God; or perhaps a better definition is that Jehovah is the self-existent one who reveals himself; he does not change in himself, but reveals himself increasingly to his people in their needs. He does not change, he is self-existent – I am that I am – but there is an extra dimension in the sense that he is manifesting and revealing himself. What a wonderful and precious promise that was when it first came to Moses. Can you imagine its effect upon him? But we must remember that we are not only thinking of Moses but also of ourselves. What God has said about himself to Moses he says to us – he is the self-existent one who is ready to reveal himself to us. We can see that if this were not true of God, if God did not reveal himself, we would know nothing about him, and we could not worship him. But he is the self-existent one who reveals himself.

But the most astounding thing about this name of God is the fact that it includes all the promises. We can put it like this. This is definitely the name of God in his relationship to man and it is particularly the name of God in the matter of redemption, which is why it is so germane to what we are discussing at the present time. There is God in his heaven in eternity and in the glory of all his qualities and perfection. And here is man on the ground. There is not only an awful difference in might and power, but there is a further terrible difference. God is holy and God is light; man is in shame and unworthiness. How can the two ever come together? The answer is that God is Jehovah – it is the name that comes to man in his sin and shame.

This is perfectly illustrated in the call of Moses. God's people, the Children of Israel, are in the captivity of Egypt. They are under cruel bondage, and are absolutely helpless. They are small in number, and they are in the hands of the mighty king, Pharaoh. How can they get out and be saved? And this is the astounding thing. We are told that God goes to a man who has been living as a shepherd for forty years, knowing himself to be a stranger in a strange land. Then God appears to him in the burning bush and he says, I am Jehovah, I am going to do something about those people, I am going to rescue them and redeem them.

It is God in the name of Redeemer, a name which includes everything connected with our redemption. He is the self-existent one who does not turn his back upon us, but looks upon us, and comes to us. He does something about us for he is Jehovah, the redeeming God. Keep your eye on that as you read the Old Testament Scriptures. This name always stands for God in his relationship to man in redemption. In other words, it is always when God is making a covenant with man that he uses it. He says to Moses, I am going to make a covenant with them, and this is the name in which I make it.

Yes, but more than that, he has condescended to break up even that name and in a sense to break it up by adding to it – if we have nothing else but this left in our minds as a result of this study we shall be the wealthiest people in the world. If only we realized what God has told us about himself in his relationship to us! Do you feel that I am being academic? If so, I am failing lamentably. What I am trying to say is that what God has revealed about himself, he has revealed *to us* – this is his relationship to us, if we but knew it. In all the names he has told us certain things about himself. Here is one great name – Jehovah-jireh. You will find it in the story of Abraham going up into that mountain to sacrifice his only son Isaac. He was on the point of striking his son when suddenly God stopped him and said, 'Do not strike him, I have another offering.' And Abraham found a ram in the thicket. The Lord had provided the offering and the sacrifice, so he gave that name, 'The Lord Will Provide'. And so, whenever you go into the presence of God, whatever your need may be, however disturbed you may be, whatever form the need may be taking, remind yourself that you are praying to Jehovah-jireh, the Lord who has promised to provide. He will be with you for he says, 'I will not fail thee, nor forsake thee' (Josh 1:5).

And then he gave another name at a time when a certain disease had broken out among the Children of Israel as they were marching from Egypt to Canaan. The whole situation seemed hopeless, but God healed them in a miraculous manner and, having done so, he gave them a name concerning himself: 'The Lord that healeth thee' (Ex 15:26). As the psalmist said, 'Bless the Lord, O my soul ... who healeth all thy diseases' (Ps 103:2–3), and by this he means that it is always in the power of God to do this. That is not to say he will always do it, but that he can and does do so when he chooses. When Paul had the thorn in the flesh, he turned to God and asked him to remove it. But it was not removed because it was not God's will in that particular case. God can heal and, in an ultimate sense, of course, he does heal all our diseases, because the ultimate disease is sin itself. It is a great promise of ultimate redemption and it does hold in embryo this further promise that is given, that the Lord Jesus Christ shall even take these bodies of ours and change them: 'Shall change our vile body' – the body of our humiliation – 'that it may be fashioned like unto his glorious body' (Phil 3:21) according to his mighty power.

There is another name which God is given: Jehovah-nissi, the Lord our Banner (Ex 17:15). That is the name he revealed to the

Children of Israel after a great victory, a victory won not by
their own strength, nor by their own military prowess, but
because God enabled them to obtain the victory – the Lord our
Banner. And you and I have enemies to meet in this world – sin
and temptation. The world is full of these subtle enemies and
behind them all is the devil himself with all his power. Do you
know what it is to be attacked by him? Do you know, for example, what it is to have blasphemous thoughts insinuated into
your minds? The saints of God have had to experience that. The
devil hurls the fiery dart, says Paul, and who are we to meet such
a foe? We are small and weak and helpless, but, thank God, we
know one whose name is Jehovah-nissi, the Lord our Banner,
who can help us smite every foe and rout and conquer every
enemy.

But then let me give you another: Jehovah-shalom – The
Lord is Peace. This was the name that God gave to Gideon who
was fearful and unhappy but God told him that he was Jehovah-
shalom (Judg 6:24), and this is one of the most precious promises. It does not matter what kind of turmoil you are in, or how
heart-sore you may be. If you are beside yourself and cannot
understand why things are happening to you, go to him. He has
promised to give you peace. Remember, too, that noble statement in Hebrews 13:20, that marvellous blessing and benedic-
tion, '...the God of peace that brought again from the dead our
Lord Jesus' – Jehovah-shalom, The Lord is Peace, he makes
peace with his people.

And then, thank God, there is that precious word which
you find in the twenty-third psalm, 'the Lord is my shepherd'
– Jehovah-ro'eh and, because of that, 'I shall not want'. Can
you say that? Do you know God like that? He has revealed
himself in that way, he is your shepherd and you need never
want in an ultimate sense. 'The Lord is my shepherd, I shall
not want.'

Then there is The Lord Our Righteousness, the name given
to Jeremiah in Jeremiah 23:6: Jehovah-tsidkenu, The Lord Our
Righteousness. And lastly, Jehovah-shammah, The Lord is
There (Ezek 48:35). He is always present. You cannot in a sense

be out of his presence because he is always there and especially in times of trouble.

I have, thus, just held these names before you, and my object in so doing is that we may remind ourselves that such is the God whom we worship and whom we adore, eternal, absolute and self-existent, but who nevertheless deigns to reveal himself to man, and those are some of the ways in which he has done so. You would have thought that this would have been enough and more than enough; you would have thought that mankind, hearing these names and having such a revelation of God through them, would have clutched at them and held on to them and that all would have been well. But such was not the case. Mankind, in spite of all this, still did not really know God and then – and this is the message of the ages, the particular message of the church – then, when man had not grasped it, this God who '... spake in time past unto the fathers by the prophets, hath in these last days spoken unto us by his son ...' who is '... the express image of his person' (Heb 1:1–3). Yes, our Lord puts it all here in these words, 'I have manifested thy name unto the men which thou gavest me out of the world' (v.6), and 'he that hath seen me hath seen the Father' (Jn 14:9).

We must leave it at that now. The Lord Jesus Christ has manifested his Father, and has manifested these names in a way that transcends everything that I have been saying. Go back to the Old Testament, look at those names, study them, read them – we are meant to do so, for they are absolutely true today. What Christ has done, in a sense, is to let the floodlight in, to open them out, and to enable us to grasp them, because he has done it in his person. Study them, and remember that what God has said is this: he is 'The Lord, The Lord God, merciful and gracious, longsuffering, and abundant in goodness and truth, keeping mercy for thousands, forgiving iniquity and transgression and sin and that will by no means clear the guilty' (Ex 34:6–7). Remember that his name is ultimately Love, that he has loved us with an everlasting love and knowing him thus, we can appropriate unto ourselves all the gracious promises. He will provide, he will heal, he will lead, he will enable us to conquer, but above all, and thank his great and holy name for this, he will never leave us nor forsake us, he will always be with us.

5

The Name of God Revealed

I have manifested thy name unto the men which thou gavest me out of the world: thine they were, and thou gavest them me; and they have kept thy word. Now they have known that all things whatsoever thou hast given me are of thee. For I have given unto them the words which thou gavest me; and they have received them, and have known surely that I came out from thee, and they have believed that thou didst send me (vv. 6–8).

At this point in our study of our Lord's prayer, let me remind you, we are concentrating in detail upon the definition which we have in these three verses of what it really means to be a Christian. Here is a description of the people for whom Christ prays and for whom alone he prays. The first thing he says about them is that they are God's people, marked out by God, chosen of God: 'Thine they were, and thou gavest them me.' And then we are interested in discovering how it is that they come into this relationship. It is originally an action of God, but how does it become actual in us? How are we to know that this is really true of us in particular?

The first thing our Lord tells us is that he has manifested the name of God to these people and they have understood it. There are two main ways, it seems to me, of looking at these three verses. You can look at them from the standpoint of what Christ has done, or from the standpoint of what the Christian believer has done – there are obviously two ultimates. Our Lord says that he has done certain things to these people and they in turn have accepted and have known assuredly these things that he has spoken clearly. The two things must go together to make a Christian. This message is proclaimed to the world and yet there are many in the world who have not believed it and are not interested in it. So the two things are essential and it is indeed very important that we should bear both these aspects in mind as we are considering this matter.

In these verses, our Lord confirms once more – and he repeats this throughout the prayer – that his supreme object in coming into the world was to manifest and to glorify the name of God. That must always be the starting point in any consideration of the Christian gospel or of salvation. I have been at pains to remind you more than once that for about the last fifty years this is surely the note that has been most seriously lacking in much of our thinking as evangelical people. Far too often we start with ourselves and end with ourselves, and with the Lord Jesus Christ. How little have we emphasized the glory and the majesty of God who is the source and fount of it all! Surely that is why so often in our religious Christian life there is so little reverence, so little awe. Our whole view is short of it, it is much too subjective. We do not start with this grand conception of the holiness of God. But that is where our Lord starts. The first thing he says when he begins to pray is, 'I have manifested thy name unto the men which thou gavest me out of the world,' because ultimately that is the end and object of salvation. Or, to use a technical term, it is the *summum bonum* of salvation.

In the Sermon on the Mount, our Lord puts it in these words, 'Blessed are the pure in heart: for they shall see God' (Mt 5:8) – that is the goal. It is our first great need and without it we can do nothing. To think that the Christian salvation ends with for-giveness or with some subjective hope of peace and joy – invaluable as these are – is to fall hopelessly short of the end and the design of salvation, which is that we might know God: 'This is life eternal, that they might know thee the only true God, and Jesus Christ, whom thou hast sent' (v. 3). This, therefore, is the greatest need of all, that we may know God, or, as our Lord puts it here, that we might know the name of God, a term which we have already considered from the Old Testament standpoint.

Now this is the greatest need because it is at this point that we are all guilty of the greatest ignorance. We talk about God, we argue about God, we express our opinions and we pray, yes, but the question is, do we *know* God, is God living to us, is he *real* to us? Is our prayer, therefore, vital? Is it a living communion and is a real transaction taking place? We all know, and we must admit it with shame, that it is the easiest thing in the world to be on our knees saying a prayer. We may do it for a long time, and yet not for a moment realize the presence of God. If you read the lives of the saints, you will find that they all emphasized this point, that the first and the most vital thing of all is always to realize the presence of God. George Müller, for example, in giving advice to a number of ministers, put that point first. He emphasized this important point that before you begin to speak at all in your prayer, you must realize the being and the presence and the reality of God.

Indeed, all the experts – if one may use such a term in such a connection – in the devotional life and in the soul's relationship to God have always emphasized that. They have said that we must take trouble about it, we must not go on to petition until we have 'recollected'. We must rid ourselves of hurry and excitement and of a desire for particular things, and we must restrain ourselves from rushing to petitions for the things we want at this particular time. Before we come to anything like that, we must realize where we are and what we are doing. We must realize in whose presence we are and to whom we are speaking, and we must remind ourselves of our relationship to him – this knowledge of God without which prayer is not real prayer. Real prayer is communion with God, it is fellowship with him, it is a conversation with God, and obviously, therefore, we must start by this active realization that we are in his presence.

Nothing, then, is more essential than that we should know the name of God. It is a terrible and a tragic thing to realize that we can be religious for a very long time and yet never really

know him, not know him as he is, not know the name of God.
Indeed, we have seen that it is quite inexcusable. God took pains
under the old dispensation to manifest himself, according to his
name, the name which he split up, the name to which he added
adjectives, in order that he might reveal himself in his great
character to the people and that they might know him.

But, because of sin, and because of man's inability and man's
incapacity, the Old Testament revelation was not enough. So
the amazing and astounding thing with which we are confronted in the New Testament is that God has now given a revelation of himself in a way that is clear and unmistakable. That
is the argument of the first verses of the epistle to the Hebrews:
'God, who at sundry times and in divers manners spake in time
past unto the fathers by the prophets, hath in these last days spoken unto us by his Son.' That is the New Testament gospel, that
is the very essence of it all. But you notice that the emphasis is
still the same. It is God who speaks, it is God's action, it is something initiated by God himself and what the Son did was to
bring us into this knowledge of himself which is the ultimate
object of salvation.

Now our Lord, therefore, having done his work, is at the
point of going back to the Father, and he sums it all up by saying, 'I have manifested thy name unto the men whom thou
gavest me out of the world.' I have done the work, he says, and
so the question is, how did he do it and how did these men know
that he had done it? How did they realize what he was doing?
And that is what our Lord himself explains to us here. He
divides it up, and puts it in different ways: 'I have manifested thy
name unto the men which thou gavest me out of the world:
thine they were, and thou gavest them me; and they have kept
thy word. Now they have known' – they have come to know
this, though they did not know it before, that is the emphasis –
'that all things whatsoever thou hast given me are of thee' – that
is part of the manifestation of the name of the Father – 'for I have
given unto them the words which thou gavest me; and they
have received them, and have known surely that I came out
from thee, and they have believed that thou didst send me.'

Thus in these various ways our Lord has manifested the name of the Father unto these people for whom he now prays.

The thing, therefore, for us to do is to consider this, and here we are looking at the very heart and centre of the gospel. Let us forget everything, if we can, for the time being. Let us forget about our personal needs and problems and all our desires and everything else. No, that is not an unkind thing to say, it is the kindest thing of all. For the teaching of Scripture is that our particular and individual personal problems will only, ultimately, be resolved as we come to know the Lord Jesus Christ, so that the most direct way to tackle them is to come to 'consider him'. If we spend our time with our problems without knowing him, we will be left with our problems, and that is why the great invitation of the epistle to the Hebrews, to a people who were in trouble is, 'Consider him' (Heb 12:3). We must not look at immediate things only, we must look at him, and as we do so and see him as he really is, as our Saviour and Mediator and Lord, all these problems will be dealt with.

Now you notice that our Lord says here that he has *manifested* the name of God unto the men whom God had given him out of the world. He does not say merely that he told them about it, he goes beyond that, he says, 'I have manifested ...' – there has been a revelation, there has been an expounding of the name. That which was concealing it has been taken away and there has been an unveiling or an unfolding – that is the meaning of the word 'manifest'. Our Lord has made the name appear, and he has put it obviously before them. This is a very rich and comprehensive term, and our Lord undoubtedly uses it deliberately so that these men who are listening to him as he prays to God might realize the variegated and manifold character of this manifestation of the name of God which he has given.

So how does the Lord Jesus Christ manifest the name of God and, especially, how does he do so in a way that is superior to the Old Testament revelation? We have been through the names, and we have seen there the wealth of the manifestation through them. Yes but here is something more. Here, as the author of the letter to the Hebrews argues, is the pre-eminence of Christ. The Old Testament was a true revelation but it was only in part and in pieces; now, in Christ, it has come in all its fullness and glory.

Here, then, our Lord's first answer is that because he is the Son of God, he has manifested the name of God in a way that nothing and no one else could ever have done. He puts that like this: 'They have received them, and have known surely that I came out from thee.' These, he says, are thy people; these are true Christians because they know that I have come out from thee. That is just another way of saying that these people have known that he is, in a unique and absolute sense, the Son of God. That is always the first thing about a Christian. There is no such thing as being a Christian unless we are perfectly clear about the person of the Lord Jesus Christ. He is, according to this revelation, the Son of God, and he is this full and final manifestation of the name of God. And because he is the Son of God, the effulgence of his nature and of his glory, the fullness of God himself – as Paul says, 'in him dwelleth all the fullness of the Godhead bodily' (Col 2:9) – it is because of this that his manifestation and revelation of the name of God is altogether superior to everything else. He is God himself in the person of his Son. 'They have known surely that I came out from thee.' 'They shall call his name Emmanuel, which being interpreted is, God with us' (Mt 1:23). It is the difference between God telling us certain things about himself and God dwelling among us in the person of the Son.

This clearly, therefore, must be a unique revelation and that is the reason why our Lord was able to say to the disciples, 'He that hath seen me hath seen the Father' (Jn 14:9) – you look at me and you see him because the Son is like the Father and partakes of the Father's nature. He is not merely saying things about the Father, he is the representative of the Father in the way that a son represents his father. A servant may be able to say everything that is right about his lord and master, he may know him well and intimately, but he can never represent him in the way that the son can. The son is a manifestation of the father by being what he is. Thus our Lord himself, while here on earth, represented and manifested the name of God in a way that is incomparable and greater than all others, because he is the Son of God. We see this in John 4, in the account of our Lord's conversation with the woman of Samaria. He had been talking about worshipping God in spirit and in truth, and on hearing his words, the woman said, 'We know that Messias cometh, which is called Christ: when he is come he will tell us all things ...' Then our Lord looked at her and said, 'I that speak unto thee am he' – Look at me, and, in a sense, you see God. And that is what he constantly repeated in many different ways.

This is a thought that is staggering in its immensity. The apostle Paul, in 2 Corinthians 1:3, says, 'Blessed be God, even the Father of our Lord Jesus Christ.' Why does he put it like that – why does he not simply say, 'Blessed be God'? Why does he describe him as 'the Father of our Lord Jesus Christ'? I once heard an old preacher give an excellent definition of this. He said, 'You may describe God as Father and it is a great term; and if you go to people and tell them that God has revealed himself as Father, you may think it conveys a very definite meaning and impression. But,' he would say, 'you have to be careful. You must not think of the term "father", or "fatherhood", as an abstract term which has no particular associations. Different people listening to the word "father" have different conceptions and ideas. You cannot assume that to say "God is Father" is going to convey a good impression to everyone, because you may be saying it to someone whose idea of "father" is of someone who is constantly under the influence of drink, someone who is blaspheming and cursing, smashing up the home, turning out his wife and children – a hateful person, a hateful term, a hateful thought. That is inevitably that poor person's idea of father because it is the only kind of father he has ever known. So,' went on the old preacher, 'that is why Paul says, "Blessed be the God and Father of our Lord Jesus Christ." As long as you remember that he is the Father of our Lord Jesus Christ, then you will never have a wrong conception of the fatherhood of God.'

In other words, we look at the Son and see what he was, and

we realize that the Father is like that. The Lord Jesus Christ is, in a sense, the Father himself appearing before us. He is not the Father, but he is the brightness, the effulgence of his glory and the express image of his person. That is the first way in which our Lord manifests the name of God. 'They have known surely that I came out from thee', and that is always one thing you know about the Christian. He knows that the Lord Jesus Christ is the only begotten Son of God, he believes in the miracle of the incarnation. He knows that Jesus was not mere man, not merely a great teacher, he is God come in the flesh: 'The Word was made flesh, and dwelt among us' (Jn 1:14). That is the belief of the Christian, he knows that, and without that there is no knowledge of God, there is no salvation.

But you notice that our Lord puts it in another form also, and how important it is that we should watch every phrase. He seems on the surface to be repeating himself, but that is not so: 'They have known surely that I came out from thee, and they have believed that thou didst send me.' Is that the same thing? Clearly, it is not. This is something different. There is a very important distinction here. The first tells us that he comes, he is the Son, the manifestation of the Father, but when he says, 'They believe that thou hast sent me', there is a further revelation of the name of God, a revelation of the peculiar, special, love of God. Yes, we start by saying that Jesus of Nazareth is the only begotten Son of God, but then we ask ourselves the question: what is he doing in this world? What is the purpose, and the object of it all?

And there is only one answer – 'God so loved the world that he gave his only begotten Son' (Jn 3:16); 'Herein is love, not that we loved God, but that he loved us, and sent his Son to be the propitiation for our sins' (1 Jn 4:10). The New Testament is full of this truth, and by emphasizing it, our Lord was revealing and manifesting the love of God in its most perfect form: 'I have manifested thy name unto the men which thou gavest me.'

How, then, did he manifest the name of God as love? He did so when he told them that he was in the world because God had sent him. It was the Father who had initiated and called him to do this. God made a covenant with him, and the fact of his coming into the world is a manifestation of the eternal heart of God as the heart of love. God had manifested his love many times in the Old Testament. You cannot read the stories there without clearly seeing his love towards those recalcitrant, rebellious Children of Israel. All that was amazing and glorious but it is nothing, I speak with reverence, when you put it into the light of this: 'He spared not his own Son', but sent him from glory into this world of sin and shame, into this rebellious, unworthy world of man. God sent his own Son, made of a woman, made under the law, because he so loved the world – we read all these great biblical statements and in that knowledge we know the love of God in a way we can never know it otherwise.

But then he also manifested the name of God by his very life and character and deportment. Read the gospels with this in mind. Look at the figure of Jesus of Nazareth and remember that you are there seeing a manifestation of the character and being and person of God. Observe his holiness, his spotless holiness, tried and tempted 'in all points like as we are, yet without sin' (Heb 4:15), walking through the mud and mire of this world yet keeping himself absolutely unspotted from it. No one could point a finger at him, no one could charge him with any fault; they tried to but he was sinless, he was absolutely perfect. The holiness of God was manifested in the perfect life and walk of his Son.

But not only that, observe, too, his hatred of sin and especially of hypocrisy. Read carefully his words spoken to the Pharisees and Scribes, see the righteous anger and indignation that fills his heart as he observes the twisting and the contortion of these hypocrites. Read the woes that he pronounced upon them, as recorded in Matthew 23. That is nothing but a manifestation of God's utter abhorrence and detestation of sin and of evil. Our God is a holy God. Yes, with all the intensity of his holy nature he hates sin and all that belongs to it. Look at the life of our Lord and you will see that he drives people out of the Temple because they are making the Father's house a house of merchandise; he pronounces his woes upon these men, and there, again, he reveals the name of God.

But thank God there is something else. We see, at the same time, his compassion, his longsuffering, his mercy, and his kindness. He was called 'the friend of publicans and sinners' and he gives again a manifestation of God by being what he was. By his character and his life he was ever revealing a great truth about God: how that, at one and the same time, God hates sin but is full of compassion towards the sinner.

And then our Lord reveals his Father not only by his life, but also by his teaching. Go through the gospels and you will find his explicit teaching about God and about his character and nature and being. And then he does the same thing by his works. Every miracle he performed was a manifestation and demonstration of the power of God, and each one, almost invariably, had the same effect upon these people. They were frightened when they saw the miracles but they glorified God, saying, 'We never saw it on this fashion' (Mk 2:12). Another time they said, 'This is the finger of God' (Lk 11:20), and indeed it was, for the works manifested the name of God. The name of God was powerful in his miracles and mighty deeds.

But, finally in these verses, we must notice the most interesting statement of all – that in verse 7. It is surely one of the most fascinating aspects of our Lord's revelation and manifestation of the name of his Father. These people, he says, 'have known that all things whatsoever thou hast given me are of thee', which surely means that our Lord is saying, in effect, 'I have shown these people and at last I have convinced them, and they have come to see that my entire ministry in this world is something that you have given me.'

With that key in your mind, go again through the four gospels, observing those extraordinary and beautiful statements of our Lord and you will find it most revealing. Here is the Son of God on earth and he says, 'The words that I speak unto you I speak not of myself' (Jn 14:10) and again, 'The word which ye hear is not mine, but the Father's which sent me' (Jn 14:24). Again, he says, 'The Father that dwelleth in me, he doeth the works' (Jn 14:10). And he is reminding us in these verses of this very thing: 'I have given unto them the words which thou gavest me.' He is here teaching that his entire ministry is something which has been given to him by God the Father. We have already considered the fact that the people have been given to him – 'Thine they were, and thou gavest them me.' Now in a sense it is not the Lord who is gathering the flock together, it is God, and he has given them to the Son. He says in verse 2 that God has 'given him power over all flesh': and he also says, 'All power is given unto me in heaven and in earth' (Mt 28:18). God has given it to him, he has given him the words to speak, he has given him the works to do, but above everything else he has given him the mediatorial office which he has come to occupy.

And finally there are those striking words of his in John 6 where he says, 'for him hath God the Father sealed' (v. 27). God has anointed him and set him apart. The disciples understood it, for in a few minutes Peter was saying they were not going to leave him for they were assured that, 'Thou art that Christ, the Son of the living God', the anointed one, the sealed one, the separated one. And that is the tremendous fact which is before us in this chapter, that all our blessed Lord came to do and all that he did, was but the carrying out of a ministry that had been given him of the Father. I am not sure but that this is not the ultimate way in which he reveals the name of the Father to us. We look at him, at his person, his life, his work, and his death upon the cross. We see it all. Yes, but do we see that it is all a ministry that is given to him of the Father? What love there must be, therefore, in the Father for him to have given the Son this wonderful office. The Son does nothing of himself. It was God the Father who determined it all. It was given to the Son to carry out, and the height of the revelation lies in that realization that it is all because God is who he is and what he is. You look at Christ, therefore, in the light of his person and work and you see there what God is. We now understand the name of God. The Old Testament terms are all suddenly illuminated, the God who is our shepherd, the God who is righteousness and justice, the God who is all powerful, the God who is peace, the God who is health – we see it all in this one person. We see all these attributes and characteristics of the almighty God in the ineffable person, portrayed and manifested before our eyes. In looking at Christ we see God, and we know God as our Father and the Father of the Lord Jesus Christ.

May God in his infinite grace grant us the enlightening of his Holy Spirit that we may so dwell upon these things, so grasp them and so realize them, that each of us shall be able to say honestly and truly, 'I do know God and I have come to know him, the only true and living God, through Jesus whom he has sent.'

6

The Christian and the Truth of God

*I have manifested thy name unto the men which thou gavest me out
of the world: thine they were, and thou gavest them me; and they
have kept thy word. Now they have known that all things whatsoever thou hast given me are of thee. For I have given unto them
the words which thou gavest me; and they have received them, and
have known surely that I came out from thee, and they have
believed that thou didst send me (vv. 6–8).*

We have seen that the teaching of the Bible is that finally nothing
really matters in this world apart from the certain and sure
knowledge that the Lord Jesus Christ is concerned about us at
this moment and interceding on our behalf, and that God himself is concerned about us and caring for us. There are many
other things with which we have to deal. We are citizens of
earthly kingdoms, we live our life in the world like everybody
else, and yet we know that all these things about which we are
rightly and legitimately concerned are things that are passing
and transient. We know that in addition to this life that we live
and share with others, there is a unique, personal life of our own
with which we shall finally be left. When all earthly scenes pass
away and the kingdoms of this world and all their pomp and
glory are as a mere nothing, we ourselves will still be there in a
state of consciousness, taking that final journey. Surely the
thing that matters, therefore, is that we should be prepared for
that and should so understand this truth that we are enabled to

live in the present and in the future, whatever may come to meet us, without being surprised, without being alarmed, without being baffled. But above all, there is nothing more important than that we should know for certain that we are the objects of God's special care and interest, and it is because this section deals with that in such a glorious and perfect manner, that we are concerned about studying it together.

Now our Lord has been telling us in these verses that the first characteristic of the people for whom he is praying is that he has revealed the name of God to them. Having in that way told us what he has done for them, he also indicates what is true of these people themselves in the light of that knowledge. There are always these two aspects: he has revealed the truth, yes, but although he has revealed it to certain persons, it has in a sense also been revealed generally to the whole world, and some people are Christians and some are not. What exactly makes the difference? Well the answer is that there is a difference in the response that is made to the revelation which has been given, and we must now consider what it is that our Lord tells us about the response which is made by those who belong to him, those who are truly Christian. In other words, when we look at what exactly it is to be a Christian, we can see here another great distinction, and I make no apology for dealing further with this subject. It seems to me that of all the words which are misunderstood in this modern world, there is none which is so misunderstood as this word 'Christian'. Some think of it purely in terms of a particular attitude towards war, others think of it in terms of a general friendliness, some vague emotion or feeling that one has on certain occasions. There are very many different views and there is indeed even a kind of paganism that often passes under the name of Christianity. This is truly appalling to contemplate, especially as one thinks of it all in the light of the Old and the New Testaments. It is vital, therefore, that we should be clear about these things, because we finally have no excuse: the revelation has been given, and we shall have to face it and give an account of what we have done with respect to it.

There is nothing, I repeat, which is more important for each one of us than to know for certain whether we are Christian or not. It is not only a matter of being able to face death, it is also a matter of being able to face life. According to the Scriptures, there is no real life apart from that which is given by the Lord Jesus Christ; everything else, apart from him, is mere existence. Though worldly success may be attached to our life and though it may lead to certain great things, ultimately it is utterly empty if it is without Christ. It does not satisfy the total personality, it leaves a great void, and there is a hunger and a thirst which nothing can satisfy save this life of God which comes to us through our Lord and Saviour Jesus Christ. That is why it is vital for us to know that we have this life. So here our Lord gives us one of his great distinctions.

These disciples, as we see very clearly from the records, were far from being perfect. They were guilty of many blunders and mistakes, they did many things which they should not have done, and they failed in a very pathetic manner right at the end when our Lord was facing the cross. Yet you notice that our Lord says certain things about them here. In spite of all their weakness and imperfection there is something about these people that differentiates them from everybody else, and it is this something that really makes them Christian. I suggest to you, therefore, that we have in these verses what we may call a kind of irreducible minimum of that which is essential for us before we have the right to apply the term Christian to ourselves.

There are certain things which are obvious on the very surface. Firstly, the thing that makes a man a Christian is something that is clearly defined and stated. People who have the idea that to be a Christian is something you cannot actually define are thereby proclaiming that they are not Christians. It is not a loose or indefinite term, it is perfectly clear and specific. The Scriptures themselves tell us to examine and prove ourselves whether we are in the faith or not, and, obviously, if we are exhorted to do that, then there must be some means by which we can do so. That is provided for us in the statement we are looking at now. It is one of the most clearly defined designations that you can ever consider.

Secondly, it is important to notice the way in which our Lord defines a Christian – it is not primarily a matter of experience. He does not talk about those people in terms of their having had a certain experience. They have had one but that is not what he puts first, that is not what he emphasizes and stresses. Neither, you observe, does he describe it in terms of some feelings which they have had. They certainly have had feelings – the Christian is aware of feelings – but that is not the way in which our Lord defines it. Neither does he put it in terms of their having taken a certain decision, or having arrived at some determination to live a better life or to do this or that. He does not define this basic demand, which is essential to being in the truly Christian position, in any one of those ways. Rather, he describes it as an attitude towards truth and especially towards the truth concerning himself.

That is, therefore, the first thing that we must emphasize: the basic, central thing about the Christian is that he is in a given relationship to the truth concerning our Lord and Saviour Jesus Christ. Now this is really one of the foundation truths and principles. Truth is obviously something that comes primarily to the mind and to the intellect, but it does not stop there, it ultimately affects the heart and the will. The Bible itself calls this particular message the truth, and clearly, therefore, it is something that comes to the whole person, to his mind and intellect, to his understanding, to his reason and to his ability to comprehend, and that is the way in which our Lord puts it here. The first thing he says about the Christian is that, 'they have kept thy word', and by using that expression 'thy word', he is describing the message, the truth, this presentation of doctrine. It comes to a man and it makes it possible for him to be a Christian.

The importance of that, of course, arises in this way: just to have a good feeling inside you does not make you a Christian. You can have that without being a Christian. Indeed, you can do a lot of good, you can hold very high and noble views and ideals and still not be a Christian, and there are many such people in the world today. They are not interested in God, nor do they believe in him; they are not interested in Christianity at all, but they are very good people. They spend much of their time trying to get rid of war and making this world a better place to live in and many other good things. I am not criticizing them. I am simply saying they are not Christians, because to have good feelings and sentiments and ideas and ambitions is not enough. The essential thing is to be definitely related to this message, to this word – 'they have kept thy word'. Our Lord then goes on to say, 'I have given unto them the words which thou gavest me.' This, therefore, is something that must come in the first position. The Christian is in a given relationship to this 'word'. This is the whole of the Christian revelation; it is the word of the gospel, the word of salvation; it is God's message to mankind. So the first thing we have to do is to ask ourselves, 'What is my relationship to that word?'

But what is this word, this message to which we are referring? Well, our Lord has analysed it into its component parts and divided it up for us, so that we shall be in no difficulty whatsoever with regard to our attitude in respect to it. He starts by telling us that the first essential message in that word which he has brought to us, is that he himself has come from God. He says, 'They ... have known surely that I came out from thee.' That is just another way of saying that the first thing that is true about the Christian is that he is clear about the person of the Lord Jesus Christ; he believes, he knows, that Jesus of Nazareth is the only begotten Son of God. That is our Lord's own definition of it (and we have already seen that this is a central theme in this prayer). A man, therefore, who is not clear about the person of the Lord is not a Christian. My first concern is not what sort of life he is living. If he regards Jesus of Nazareth as only a man, he is not a Christian. The Christian believes in the incarnation, he believes that almost two thousand years ago the Son of God came into this world and entered into time, 'The Word was made flesh, and dwelt among us.' He does not say that that is irrelevant, or that he believes in the Christian dogma but that the great thing for him is how to get rid of this or that international problem. The Christian cannot speak like that because to the Christian the most momentous fact in the whole of history is the incarnation of the Son of God. It towers in importance over and above the conquest of Julius Caesar; it is altogether more important than all the world wars put together. These things have their significance, but when you put them in the light of the incarnation even they pale into nothing. This is the most vital thing in life and history.

The Christian is, of course, interested in those other things, but only in the light of this central fact, this momentous thing which took place when the eternal Son of God was born as a babe in a stable in Bethlehem and put in swaddling clothes there in a manger. That is the first thing in this word, that Christ speaks about. It is the word about himself, that he has come forth from God. He is not a man like other men, for he was not born in a natural manner. It was a virgin birth, a miraculous birth, the unique event of all history, the great watershed of time determining the whole of human existence. Are we quite certain about the person of the Lord Jesus Christ? Do we know for certain that he is the only begotten Son of God? Do we accept this record concerning him? Do we believe it, because, let me repeat, if we do not, we are not Christian, it is the first, absolute, essential.

Then he goes on to emphasize the second thing which is, 'they believed also that thou didst send me'. Now that is a different thought from the one which we have been considering and our Lord separates them for a reason. Did you notice how he links up these various thoughts and concepts with the word 'and'? There is a distinction, the word covers them all but these are the component parts. The Christian, having believed that Jesus of Nazareth is the only begotten Son of God, also believes that God has sent him and commissioned him to come into this world. We have already seen this from the standpoint of our Lord himself and his work, and how marvellous this is! And this again differentiates between the Christian and the non-Christian in this world. Everybody who is not a Christian looks at the problems of mankind and of the whole world just along the human level – what can be done about it? What arrangements can be made? What can be done at the next conference? What party are you going to put into office in order that these problems may be solved? They are looking at the problems from that level only and they are trusting to the ingenuity of man somehow to deal with the situation. But the Christian does not look at it like that; the Christian knows that God is interested in this world, and that he has done something about it, in that he has intervened in the history of mankind.

In other words, to the Christian there are two types of history, whereas to the non-Christian there is only one, and that is human history – what men do and arrange. But to the Christian there is another type of history, also, which is what God has been doing. You will find these two types of history in the Bible. Sometimes they have no connection with one another, then they come nearer, until they coincide. They coincide at the incarnation when eternity came into time and God was made flesh. But the great principle to hold on to is that God has sent his Son into this world, 'God so loved the world, that he gave his only begotten Son.' We are not left with mere man, we are not just left with the world as it is. In addition to human history, there is this other dimension, and as you look at the whole course of history in the light of this event of God sending his Son, it gives you an entirely new view of the world of time, of the future, and of all things. It does not leave us on the horizontal level, but enables us to see a new possibility. The Christian believes that Christ came into the world because God sent him there.

But, thirdly, perhaps this is best put in terms of the statement in the seventh verse: 'Now they have known that all things whatsoever thou hast given me are of thee', which is just another way of stating that there is a great plan of salvation, and that the Christian is a man who knows something about this plan. The Christian is not someone who has a feeling in a meeting and then goes to the penitent form or to the decision room without knowing why he has done so. The apostle Peter says that as Christians we should be ready at all times to give a reason for the hope that is in us (1 Pet 3:15). The Christian, therefore, is not merely a man who says, 'I feel wonderful, I have marvellous new life, and I am filled with hope.' For if someone else asks him what his hope is based upon, or someone says, 'Why do you feel like this? What has given you this feeling?' and he cannot answer that question, he is not a Christian.

As I understand my New Testament, the Christian is able, however falteringly, to give a reason for the hope that is in him, because he knows the plan of salvation. He knows that God has appointed his Son to be the Saviour. These disciples for whom Christ was praying, and whom he described in this manner, were very imperfect and full of faults. But there was one thing they knew, and that was that he was the Messiah, the Saviour. On one occasion, when our Lord asked his disciples if they also were going to leave him, Peter replied, 'To whom shall we go? thou hast the words of eternal life. And we believe and are sure that thou art that Christ, the Son of the living God' (Jn 6:68–69). With all their faults and imperfections they knew that God had sent him to be the Saviour of the world, and that his words were not those of a mere man, but the words of eternal life. The Christian is the man who has come to see and to know that God sent his Son into this world to bear the sins of many, that he has come to give his life a ransom for many. There is only one way of knowing God and knowing that your sins can be forgiven. It can only be because the Son of God came into this world and took them upon himself. He bore their punishment – that is what the Christian knows.

And he knows likewise that Christ is the bread of life, that he gives him new life, new power, and a new understanding. He lives on Christ, who, himself, has told him that he must eat the flesh and drink the blood of the Son of Man. This means that he depends upon Christ and draws his life from him. He is in that intimate relationship with Christ. The Christian knows that and believes it, says our Lord. That is the word which the Christian believes – the whole plan of salvation.

If that, then, is the truth which the Christian is to believe, what is his peculiar relationship to that truth, for that, after all, is our basic definition of a Christian? Again, our Lord has answered the question in these three verses. What a perfect analysis this is of faith, what an incomparable analysis of the relationship of the Christian to truth. This is a great and profound subject. I merely note it to you, for your own meditation, but each word and each step is vital. The whole is there, of course, but our Lord breaks it up for us into these component parts.

Let me just give you the headings. What is the relationship of the Christian to this message, to this word of God that has come into the world? The first thing we are told about the Christian is that he is *one who receives*: 'I have given unto them the words which thou gavest me; and they have received them.' Our Lord was drawing a contrast here between the disciples and those who rejected the word, those who always criticized and ridiculed it, or who were always arguing about it – read the gospels and you will see what I mean. Our Lord there often uttered many gracious words, but the Pharisees' response was to look at one another and say, Who is this man who is teaching in this way? He is only a carpenter's son, the son of Joseph and Mary. He has no learning. He has not even been to the schools. And so they argued with him and tried to trap him. That is the opposite of receiving the word, because to receive it means to appropriate it in your heart.

There is a great illustration of this in Acts 17. We read there of certain people who lived in a place called Berea and who, when they heard the word, were ready to listen to it and went to the Scriptures to confirm it. That is the attitude of receiving, and obviously this is the first thing that is true about the Christian, the thing that differentiates him from the non-Christian. He accepts the word. He is not like others who are always trying to find holes in the argument, or to discover a contradiction in it, or who, if they hear that someone, some dignitary perhaps, has cast doubts upon the faith, are ready to believe him and to question the truth. No, Christians receive and accept. Often there may be things about the truth that they do not understand, but they believe that this is the Son of God, they listen to him, they receive his word, and give it a real place in their heart. They are open to it.

Then the next thing is '*they have believed*'. There is a difference between receiving and believing. Believing is, I would say, a step forward. It means that not only is there an openness to the word and a general state of receptivity, but, beyond that, it has been literally taken hold of – which is much more specifically faith. Belief, then, appropriates the word, it grasps it and says, 'I believe it. I am not only open to receive it, I listen, and I accept it. I commit myself to it because I know it is right.' 'They have believed,' says our Lord, 'that thou didst send me.' That was even used as a confession in the early church, like the confession of Peter at Caesarea Philippi. People were saying that our Lord was John the Baptist, Elijah, Jeremiah or one of the prophets, so he asked his disciples, 'Whom say ye that I am?' And Peter's answer was, 'Thou art the Christ, the Son of the living God' (Mt 16:13–17) – we believe that.

Then the next term he uses is the term 'know'. 'Now *they have known* that all things whatsoever thou hast given me are of thee.' He says, 'They have received them [the words], and *have known surely* that I came out from thee.' This again is obviously another stage forward. There is a sense, of course, in which faith and knowledge cannot be separated. The relationship between them is a great question for discussion and in one sense they cannot be separated. There is always a kind of certainty about faith, not a certainty that you can prove scientifically, but an absolute certainty – 'faith is the substance of things hoped for' (Heb 11:1). Paul uses the great word 'I am persuaded' – I am sure – and there is, therefore, this kind of sequence in the attitude of the Christian towards truth. He receives it, he believes it and then he comes to know it. From believing he gets assurance, and he is as certain of the truth as he is of anything in existence, if not more so. It is very difficult to put these things into words but one of the greatest blessings of being in the Christian position is that one is really assured about these things. It is not an assurance that you can generate for yourself, but one that is always produced by the Holy Spirit. It is his peculiar work to do that, and to the man who wants to believe he will give the knowledge. Then he will give the assurance and so we advance from reception, to belief, to knowledge and to assurance.

And that brings me to my last point, a wonderful description of faith which our Lord puts first because it includes all the others: 'they have *kept* thy word.' What does it mean? In the first place, it means an intent watching, an observing of the whole revelation. You cannot keep a thing unless you have your eye on it, as it were, and therefore a good definition of the Christian is that he is a man who has always kept his eye on the truth. In every realm and department of life this is the thing that really controls him. He does not merely think of it and try to concentrate on it, and then forget it – not at all! His eye is always on the truth. The revelation is to him the great thing in life and he keeps it ever before him. It is a fundamental attitude which is always true of the Christian, always looking at the whole truth and meditating upon it – the word carries the meaning of watching. 'They have kept thy word.'

There were many who seemed to have received it but who did not keep it, as we see in John 6. These people were following our Lord in crowds because they had seen his miracle of the feeding of the five thousand. They thought it was wonderful and they had never seen anything like it before; our Lord had become 'the latest craze'. Having seen the miracle, they crowded after him and then he began to preach to them. But when he began to tell them that they must eat his flesh and drink his blood and live on him, they stood back and said, 'This is an hard saying; who can hear it?' And they went back and walked no more with him – they had not kept his word. But his disciples were different and, as we saw earlier, it was then that Peter made his great statement – 'To whom shall we go? ...' There is no one to go to, says Peter. We cannot always understand you, you are an enigma, but we will not leave you. They had kept the word, they held on to it through thick and thin. They did not allow others and their difficulties to loose their hold of him; they did not allow the devil to shake their belief, nor did they allow the detraction of the world to keep them away. They put the word in their heart, as the psalmist said, 'Thy word have I hid in mine heart, that I might not sin against thee' (Ps 119:11). Those people were guarding it, watching it, so that nothing should succeed in an attempt to take it from them.

And the last meaning of this word – you will find this rendering in other translations – is that they *obeyed* God's word, because finally you do not really keep the word of God unless you obey it. It is a word that cannot be kept only in your intellect; it has to be put in your heart and in your will also. The man who keeps the word of God is the man whose whole personality is keeping it, the man who is meditating and rejoicing in it, whose heart warms to it, and so he obeys it.

I sum it all up, therefore, by putting it like this: ultimately the Christian is a man who realizes that in this life and world nothing really matters but this truth of God, this truth about the Lord Jesus Christ. He knows that Christ is the Saviour of his soul, the Saviour of the world, the one who has been, the one who has gone, the one who will come again. He is the one who will come on the clouds of heaven as King of kings and Lord of lords and rout his every enemy and rid the world of sin and evil and introduce that blessed, glorious state in which there shall be 'new heavens and a new earth, wherein dwelleth righteousness' (2 Pet 3:13). That is the Christian, the man whose life is dominated and controlled by that truth, who keeps himself in every realm by that word, which comes to his mind, moves his heart and exercises his will. He lives by the truth of God as it is to be found only in our blessed Lord and Saviour Jesus Christ.

My beloved friends, are you keeping this word? Are you safeguarding it, holding on to it, practising and living it? That is the one thing that matters. And if you have kept this word – well, then, blessed be his name, you can be certain that he will keep you.

7

Christ Glorified in Us

And I am glorified in them (v. 10).

As we consider these words it will be well for us also to bear in mind verse 18 which reads: 'As thou hast sent me into the world, even so have I also sent them into the world.'

In dividing up this section which runs from verses 6–19, we indicated, you remember, that there are two main divisions. Our Lord is here praying for his own immediate followers. First of all he gives the reasons why he prays for them, and then he brings his specific petitions to his Father's notice. At the moment we are dealing with the reasons which he adduces for praying for his own, and for a number of studies we have been considering the first reason, which is given in verses 6–8. He prays for these people because they are who and what they are, and we have worked that out in detail.

We come now to our Lord's second reason for praying for them. He prays for them because of what they are meant to do, because of their calling and their task; and that is stated here in this phrase at the end of verse 10. Having described them, having enumerated the things that characterize them, he now reminds his followers of their function and their business in this world of time, and he puts that in the remarkable phrase which we are now considering. He says that as his Father had sent him into the world, even so he has sent them into the world (v. 18). God, we have seen, in sending the Son, had a specific object in

79

view, that the Son should do certain things, and the greatest of them all was to glorify his Father. Now here our Lord says that he has sent, and does send, his people into the world, in exactly the same way as God had sent him, and the great task and function of his people is to glorify him.

Now our Lord said many things about those of us who are Christians, but I am sure you will agree that this particular statement is one of the most amazing – indeed staggering – of all, and it is one which is obviously full of real significance for us. Observe, for instance, the sequence in which this statement comes, and the context in which we find it in this chapter. Our Lord himself, he tells us here in this prayer, glorifies his Father. There in the heavens is the Father, God in his ultimate being and essence, and the Son of God has come into the world to glorify him. That is the first step.

Then the next step is that the Holy Spirit has been sent in order that he may glorify the Son. We are shown this abundantly in the chapters leading up to this seventeenth chapter, which you remember starts like this: 'These words spake Jesus, and lifted up his eyes to heaven, and said…' and then follows the prayer. The phrase 'these words' refers to chapters 14, 15 and 16, in which you have that great teaching about the Holy Spirit, his person and his work. It can all be summed up like this: he does not speak of himself or about himself. The peculiar function and purpose of the Holy Spirit is to reveal, to manifest and therefore to glorify the Son.

But you notice that it does not stop at that. The next step is this phrase that we are looking at here. The result of the coming of the Holy Spirit and his entering into the believer, and into the believer's life, is that the believer also glorifies the Son. 'I am glorified in them,' he says, and he sends them to do this specific work. Thus at once we find here that those of us who are Christians are brought into this very sequence – the sequence which contains the blessed Holy Trinity. Everything is for the glory of God. The Son has come, he speaks, he lives, he dies, he does everything to that end. The Spirit glorifies the Son and we, as the result of the operation of the Spirit, also glorify him. It is, indeed, a staggering thought and conception.

Again, you can look at it from the standpoint of the Lord Jesus Christ himself being glorified. You remember that at the beginning of the prayer we found that he asked that his Father would glorify him.[1] 'Father,' he says, 'the hour is come; glorify thy Son, that thy Son also may glorify thee.' The teaching is, therefore, that the Father does glorify the Son. The Son is the centre, the Father glorifies him from heaven, and, as we have said, the Holy Spirit also glorifies him. He has been sent to do so, and we read in those early chapters of Acts how Peter in his preaching explains clearly that that is the work of the Holy Spirit. We find it put still more specifically in chapter 5, where the apostle says, 'We are his witnesses of these things; and so is also the Holy Ghost, whom God hath given to them that obey him' (Acts 5:32). So here we see the Son in the centre with the light and the radiance of the Father upon him to glorify him; then we see the light of the Holy Spirit, too, focussed upon him, revealing him in his glory and in all his splendour. But the remarkable, almost incredible, thing is that you and I also are called to do exactly the same thing: to glorify the Son.

Here is something that really does come to us in a most amazing way, that the one who is glorified by the almighty Father in heaven, and by the blessed Holy Spirit with all his power, should also be glorified by us, and through us. Our Lord says this quite specifically, and it is something which is taught concerning the Christian right through the New Testament. Take, for instance, the way in which the apostle Peter puts it in his first epistle where he makes precisely this same point: 'But ye are a chosen generation, a royal priesthood, an holy nation, a peculiar people' – why? – 'that ye should show forth the praises' – the virtues, the excellencies – 'of him who hath called you out of darkness into his marvellous light' (1 Pet 2:9). That is Peter's description of the Christian, that is what we are here for. Our business is to manifest, to make a display of, the glories and the power of our Lord Jesus Christ.

[1] See *Saved in Eternity* (Kingsway Publications 1988).

And the apostle Paul in Ephesians 3:10 says very much the same thing: 'To the intent that now unto the principalities and powers in heavenly places might be known by the church the manifold wisdom of God' – it is by means of, or through, the church, that these principalities and powers are really going to be given a view and an insight into God's wisdom. In a sense it seems ridiculous that these bright angelic spirits who are constantly in God's presence, could be helped in any way by the church, but it is through the church that they come to know this manifold, many-sided wisdom of God. That is the teaching, and therefore it brings us, at once, face to face with one of the most remarkable definitions of the Christian that is to be found even in the realm of Scripture itself.

Now we must pause for a moment at this point, just so that we may consider the privilege of being a Christian. Let us look at the fact that you and I are put into a position in which Christ can be glorified in us – for that is precisely what we are told. But how sadly lacking we are in this realization of our privilege. Everybody is interested in privileges; the newspapers are full of it. People are fighting for them, they will spend fortunes in order to get a certain privilege and position, or to hold on to one. But is there anything that the world has ever known which is in any way comparable to this? All the pomp and greatness and ceremony of the world just vanish into utter insignificance by the side of what is said here about any and every Christian: namely that to us is given this astounding privilege of glorifying the Lord Jesus Christ, that he, the Son of God, the effulgence and brightness of the Father's face, should be glorified in us.

Or think of it for a moment from the standpoint of our responsibility as Christians. Whether we are fully aware of it or not, the fact is that the Lord says here that he is glorified in his people. Anybody, therefore, who professes and claims the name of Christian is in this sense a custodian of the name, the glories and the virtues of the Lord Jesus Christ, and through him of God himself. That is the responsibility of a Christian. An ambassador from any country is always conscious of the fact that he has a tremendous responsibility because he is the representative by whom his country is going to be judged. And to us is given the privilege and the responsibility of being the representatives of the Son of God in this world. We stand for him, people judge him by what they see in us, and they are perfectly entitled to do so because we are the ones through whom and in whom he is glorified. Do we, I wonder, always realize this?

But then let us also look at it like this: there is surely nothing, it seems to me, that so helps us to rise to the height of our great calling as the realization of this very thing. As I have said before, our main trouble as Christians is that we do not realize the truth about our position. Our further trouble is that we do not realize who and what we are, what we are meant to be, and what we are meant to do. Now the way in which the New Testament teaches sanctification and holiness is just to hold these things before us constantly, and it seems to me that the 'holiness' teaching which concentrates on the experiences which one receives is completely false. The New Testament comes and says, do you realize who you are? Do you realize that Christ is glorified in you? Do you realize that you are his representative here on earth and that all this responsibility and privilege is yours?

Then, having told us that, the Bible puts certain questions to us. It says, in view of this can you possibly continue being slack as a Christian? Can you be negligent in your Christian duties? Can you take these things lightly and loosely, scarcely ever giving them a thought? The man who is representing his family or his nation among other people is very careful to remind himself of that fact; he is always careful to remind himself, daily, of the responsibility that is upon him and of the consequences of his possible failure. I wonder how often we stop and just say to ourselves, 'Now because I am a Christian I am going to be a representative of Jesus Christ. Christ is going to be glorified in me; that is my business. I cannot afford to be slack, or to take these things for granted, nor can I afford to give my time and energy and my spare time to things which I know are of no ultimate value.' Surely if we realized this it would immediately correct any tendency to indolence or slackness in our Christian lives.

Or look at it in this way. We are told here by the Lord himself, 'I am glorified in them' – they are the people who are expressing my glories, my excellencies and my virtues. But let us look at them, miserable, uncertain about themselves and their position, afraid, perhaps, that certain of their friends or their superiors should know that they are Christians at all, apologizing almost for it – is that not the picture which we far too often present, without enthusiasm, without zeal? We see other people getting excited even about such things as football matches, shouting for their side, wearing colours so that everybody may know which side they support. We see people boasting about all kinds of things in this life and world. Yet when we come to our Christianity and Christian profession, oh, how often we lack enthusiasm and energy, and pride in being what we are. Instead of proclaiming it to the whole world, we conceal it or are uncertain about it and even present the aspect of being defeated, and so on. If this is true of us, then surely there is only one explanation for it and that is that we do not realize that Christ is glorified in us. We have never realized the truth about ourselves, nor the privilege and the responsibility of our exalted position. We have never realized truly that we are the children of God and joint heirs with Christ – the children of the heavenly King. But the moment we do realize this, it becomes a corrective to us.

In the same way, that is surely how to conquer sin, and to overcome temptation and evil. If only we would remind ourselves in the moment of temptation that we are the representatives of Christ, and that it is through us that his glories are to be manifested. Is there anything that is so likely to make us withstand and avoid temptation as the realization of this wonderful thing? *That* is how the New Testament calls us to behave, that is what we are to be, worthy of our calling – 'Be ye holy; for I am holy,' says God himself (1 Pet 1:16). This therefore is the thing to which we are called. Christ sends us into the world in order that we may glorify him. Again I ask my question – are we doing that? Is he being glorified in us? Do people think well and highly of him because they know us and because of the way in which we represent him? I am not surprised that he prayed for his disciples – God knows we need his prayers. He knows the task to which he is sending his people and he knows his people. So he prays to his Father for us, and I thank God that he is interceding on my behalf at the right hand of God's glory at this moment.

How does the Christian glorify Christ? How is it possible for us, evil creatures as we are, to add in any way a kind of glory or lustre to his name? The answer is given very freely here in this chapter and indeed everywhere in the New Testament. Our Lord has already been dealing with one way in which we glorify him: we do so by believing in him. He says here about these people that they have glorified him already because they recognized who he was. The world in general did not, nor did the Pharisees, who called him 'this fellow', 'the carpenter', and 'the son of Joseph and Mary'. The apostle Paul tells us that the princes of this world did not recognize the Lord of glory, for if they had, they would not have crucified him (1 Cor 2:8). Because he was born in humiliation, because he came in a particular way, the great and noble and the mighty of the world did not recognize him. Therefore they did not glorify him, or worship him, nor did they praise him. It was his own people who recognized that he was the Son of God. And you and I, by believing in the Lord Jesus Christ, glorify him. To recognize him as the incarnate Son of God, to believe that he has come into this world in the flesh and has lived amongst us in the likeness of sinful flesh – that, in and of itself, is to glorify him.

But we go beyond that. It means that we recognize also why he came and what he has done in this world. To glorify Christ, says the apostle Paul in 1 Corinthians, is to recognize in him the wisdom and the power of God. To the Jews, he says, he is a stumbling block, and to the Greeks he is foolishness, but 'unto them which are called, both Jews and Greeks, Christ the power of God, and the wisdom of God' (1 Cor 1:24). This means that the Lord Jesus Christ is God's way of salvation. And the way in which he desires to be glorified by men is that they should recognize that he is the way in which God is bringing men to a knowledge of himself, reconciling them unto himself, and preparing for himself this special people. So anybody who recognizes that is glorifying the Lord Jesus Christ, and this includes, too, recognizing the love that made him do it all, the love that brought him into this world and made him suffer the contradiction of sinners against himself, and, above all, the love that took him freely and readily to the cross that he might die for us and purchase our pardon and forgiveness and make us one with God.

All that, but especially our recognition of the meaning of the cross, is a part of the way in which we glorify the Lord. This is why so many of our hymns deal with it: 'In the cross of Christ I glory'. 'God forbid that I should glory, save in the cross of our Lord Jesus Christ,' says Paul in Galatians 6:14, and the hymn echoes it. Or, again,

> When I survey the wondrous cross,
> On which the Prince of Glory died,
> My richest gain I count but loss,
> And pour contempt on all my pride.
> *Isaac Watts*

And I pour contempt on everything else that I have ever gloried in. The cross is the only thing in which we should glory; I recognize what is happening there and I know that the Son of God has come down to earth and has come down to that cross, in order that I might be forgiven and that I might be made a child of God. In believing in him in this way I glorify him, and it is my desire that I should do so.

Or, again, we glorify him by asserting that he is everything to us. He has chosen to save mankind, says Paul again, in 1 Corinthians 1, and our only response to that must be 'He that glorieth, let him glory in the Lord' (1 Cor 1:31). The Christian, by definition, is a man who says, 'I am nothing, I am what I am entirely by the grace of God.' He is a man who is always flying to Christ, and one who disclaims anything in and of himself. He has come to an end of his self-reliance, the world has been crucified to him and he has been crucified to the world; he glories in the cross and in Christ alone.

But obviously this implies that we glorify the Lord Jesus Christ by telling other people about him, by pointing them to his glory and by trying to bring them also to glorify him and to glory in his cross. Now that is where verse 18 is so important: 'As thou hast sent me into the world, even so have I also sent them into the world.' And he has sent us into the world, that we might tell the world about him. Acts chapter 4 brings this out very clearly, and it is equally striking in chapter 3. We read the story of Peter and John going up to the Temple, and there seated at the Beautiful Gate of the Temple is the lame beggar. Then we are told that Peter and John fastened their eyes upon him and said: 'Look on us,' and when he looked at them Peter said, 'Silver and gold have I none; but such as I have give I thee: In the name of Jesus Christ of Nazareth rise up and walk.' And the man, we are told, went with them into the Temple, walking, and leaping, and praising God. Here the crowd gathered, full of curiosity, and were on the point of worshipping the apostles, but Peter turned to them and said, 'Why marvel ye at this? or why look ye so earnestly on us, as though by our own power or holiness we have made this man to walk?' Why look on us? It is not us, but, 'The God of our fathers hath glorified his Son Jesus ... And his name through faith in his name hath made this man strong, whom ye see and know: yea, the faith which is by him hath given him this perfect soundness in the presence of you all' (vv 12–13, 16). Peter pointed them to Christ and preached Christ to them.

And the apostles did exactly the same thing when they were brought before the Council – you will find the record in the fourth chapter of Acts. They just looked at those religious leaders and said it was nothing that they had done, 'for there is none other name under heaven given among men, whereby we must be saved' (v. 12). They pointed to him, they preached the name of Jesus, and then they continued and said, 'We cannot but speak the things which we have seen and heard.' They were always proclaiming Christ, telling people that he is the Son of God, the anointed of God, the Saviour of the world, the one to whom everyone must go if they desire salvation. And thus, of course, the whole time, they were glorifying him, they were holding him up as it were, they were flashing this light on to him, and saying, There he is, look at him, believe in him. They were pointing the whole world to Jesus Christ.

Now that is what we are called upon to do; we are meant to talk to people about the Lord Jesus Christ and to tell them he is the Son of God and that he has come into this world in order to save men and women. We are meant to tell them in the midst of all these exciting discussions about politics and these various other things, that ultimately there is no hope for the individual, or for society, apart from this blessed person. We are meant to tell men exactly why the world is as it is; we are meant to tell them about sin in the human heart and that nobody and nothing can deal with it save the Son of God. That is how we glorify him, by talking about him. We are very ready to talk about our doctors, and to praise the man who cured us when so many failed; we talk about some business which is better than others, or about films and plays and actors and actresses, and a thousand and one other things. We are always glorifying people, the world is full of it, and the Christian is meant to be praising and glorifying the Lord Jesus Christ. Speaking to his Father here in John 17, he says, 'I have glorified thee' but the world laughs at me, the world ridicules me, especially my dying upon the cross. My whole reputation is in the hands of these people. Father, he says, look upon them, keep them, I am glorified in them, they are my representatives in the world. If they do not speak about me there, who will? If they do not praise me, who can? I am glorified only in them.

And that obviously leads to the next point, which is that we glorify him by being what we are. Or, to put it another way, we glorify him in that we are living proofs and examples of the truth of what he has said about us. I think that this is tremendously important. I rather like to think of the Christian in this way, and I apply this test to myself. Unless I am giving the impression that I am what I am only because of the Lord Jesus Christ, to that extent I am failing as a Christian. I mean that as a Christian, I am to be the kind of person of whom people say, 'What is it about this man? We cannot explain him.' And they will never be able to explain him until they discover that the secret of this man is that Christ is in him.

I wonder whether this is how people think of us. I wonder whether we can be adequately explained in terms of temperament – that we are undoubtedly the sort of people who would always be interested in religion. If so, we are not glorifying Christ because you can be religious without being a Christian at all; you can be interested in religion and in God and still not be a Christian. Religion can be explained quite easily apart from Christ, and, by definition, the Christian is the man who can only be explained in terms of Christ.

Or can we be explained in terms of our training? People say, 'Oh yes, it is their tradition, they have a sense of loyalty to it, and to the Christian church. There is no difficulty about explaining what they do, they have been brought up to it.' Well, if they can explain us like that, we are not Christian, in this sense because Christ is not being glorified in us.

Or can they explain us in terms of self-government? 'He is rather striking,' they say. 'He has his own moral code, and we expect him to do the things he does, and to refrain from doing others.' Now, if I can be explained like that or in any one of those ways, I say that to that extent I am not glorifying Christ.

No, we glorify Christ in this way. People meeting with us say, 'What is it about them? Our explanations and our categories are of no value, there is something else, there is something mysterious, there is another thing.' That is what they should be saying. The Lord Jesus Christ when he was here in this world, by being what he was, glorified God. People were baffled by him. They saw his miracles and the effect was almost invariably that they glorified God. They said, 'We have never seen things in this way before.' By doing what he did, he glorified God. And you and I are to be exactly like that. We are to be such people that the moment people meet us they think about Christ. We are told a very significant thing in the fourth chapter of the Acts of the Apostles. The Council that was trying the apostles could not understand them. They observed that they were ignorant men and yet the fact was that they had performed a miracle and were speaking in a manner which could not be accounted for. And then we are told that they took note of the fact that they had been with Jesus – it seemed to be the only explanation. And that is the test of a Christian; he cannot be explained apart from Jesus Christ, and thereby he glorifies him.

But we must go beyond this. We glorify him by saying what he has done to us, and by what he has made of us. We are the manifestation of his power. We glorify him by showing that we have been separated from the world. 'I pray for them: I pray not for the world,' says our Lord, and the mere fact that you and I have been separated, set apart from the world, is in and of itself a proof of the power of Christ, the Son of God. There is nothing that can really bring a man out of the world and its mentality but the power of Christ; but he does, he separates us and he makes us different. The man, therefore, who is different is the man who is glorifying Christ. Now I know perfectly well that when I say that, I am saying something that the modern Christian, speaking generally, does not like. The modern Christian has for some time been going out of his way to be as much like the world as he can. His great idea is that he can affect the mannerisms of the particular society to which he belongs, and incidentally be a Christian. But, though he thinks that he is bearing a marvellous testimony, it is a little difficult to find out whether or not he is a Christian.

Now the New Testament always emphasizes the exact opposite. It teaches that the Christian is a man who strikes you at once as being different. He has something about him that nobody else has; he has got something of Christ himself about him, with none of this modern self-assertion and confidence and pride which so often pass for personality. No, the Christian belongs to the meek and lowly Jesus; he belongs to one, who, though he was the prince of glory, had no place, on this earth, where he could lay his head. He was the one of whom it is said, 'A bruised reed shall he not break, and the smoking flax shall he not quench' (Is 42:3). The Christian has been separated and taken out of the world with its mentality and outlook. He stands by the side of Christ, and there is something of the radiance and glory of his Master and Lord and Saviour about him.

But the Father has not only separated us in general, he has made us spiritually alive. Whereas those who are not Christians are not interested in spiritual things, the Christian is. The world is not interested in the affairs of the soul at all and tries to avoid considering them. The world is spiritually dead, dead in trespasses and sins and it regards spiritual things as utterly boring. It wants to enjoy the world, it is out for the glittering prizes that the world has to offer. But the Christian has been made spiritually alive. He is very concerned about the affairs of the soul, they are the things that come first in his life and in all his thinking. How then has this happened? It is the power of Christ that has come upon him: 'You hath he quickened, who were dead in trespasses and sins' (Eph 2:1). We have been quickened together with Christ and raised up with him and he has given us a new life and a new understanding, a new outlook upon everything. And thus, by manifesting in our lives the power of Christ, we are glorifying him – if I may use such a term – we are adding lustre to his name for all who know us and come into contact with us. And we are what we are because the power of Christ has taken hold of us. We are different, we are changed, we have become new men, and the extent to which we give that impression is the extent to which we are glorifying Christ.

You will see that obviously I have not exhausted this subject. The questions with which we need to confront ourselves and by which we must examine and test ourselves are these. Is he being glorified in me? Am I representing my Father? Am I testifying in various ways about him? Not that I become a busybody just buttonholing people in a mechanical manner and asking them, 'Are you saved?' No, but testifying for him by singing his praises and by doing it with the wisdom of a serpent and yet being as gentle as a dove, and, yes, always pointing to him. And I glorify him especially by being what I am, an enigma and a problem to all who do not know Christ, because my life can, more and more, be described in this way: 'I live; yet not I, but Christ liveth in me' (Gal 2:20), or 'By the grace of God I am what I am' (1 Cor 15:10). Oh the privilege of this position, the responsibility of this position and the high calling to which Christ has called us, that he himself should be glorified in us.

8

Manifesting the Work of Christ

I am glorified in them (v. 10).

In our last study we saw that there is nothing that so urges us to a life of holiness and devotion to God as the realization that the Lord Jesus Christ is glorified amongst men in us and through us. We know that the world is antagonistic and that it is not interested in him; and the world is judging him and is estimating him by what it sees in us. So often we have met people who are not Christians and who never go near a place of worship, and the reason they immediately give for this is – 'Look at So and So!' It is because of something they have seen in a church member or someone who calls himself or herself a Christian, and they have been judging the Lord Jesus Christ by what they have seen in this person. Now that is just a negative way of putting what our Lord here puts positively: 'I am glorified in them', because, thank God, the other side can also be presented. There are people who were once not Christians, and who were, indeed, antagonistic to Christianity, who are in the Christian church today because they were arrested by something that they saw in a Christian person.

I heard recently about a candidate who offered herself to a certain missionary society, and her story was that she had not only been a Communist herself, but she had also been the Secretary of the Communist Society in her university. And the thing that arrested that girl and started the whole process of her conversion was, not a sermon, not an address, not a book on apologetics, nor an intellectual argument, but the simple observation of the daily life and walk of a fellow student. Intellectually that other student was not fit to be put into the same category as this Communist, but what she beheld in that girl's life and walk so arrested and so condemned her, and she was so charmed by it, that eventually she became a Christian herself – 'I am glorified in them.' So this is obviously one of the most important things we can ever consider together. We are called to this, this is our peculiar function as Christian people.

What, then, are we called to do? Perhaps we can sum it up like this: we are meant to be a living proof of the fact that the Lord Jesus Christ has finished the work which his Father sent him to do. As he has already reminded us in his prayer, the Father sent him into the world to do a certain task: 'I have glorified thee on the earth: I have finished the work which thou gavest me to do,' he says, and I look to them – to the Christians – to manifest this.

The world, as we have seen, does not believe in him nor in his message. The main object of the devil – the antagonist of God and his Christ – is always to ridicule both the Christian message and the Lord himself. The devil is boldly, actively engaged in the world all the time and it is astonishing to know the way in which the devil is increasingly opposing the Lord Jesus Christ and his work. The world, in its whole outlook and life, with its suggestions, its innuendoes and its ridicule, is always trying to prove that he is not the Son of God. The devil has achieved nothing but evil, and because of that there is nothing in the world now to manifest the truth but the testimony and the witness and the life of Christian people. It is by us and by us alone that he is glorified in this world.

We have begun to consider how we do this and now I want to come to the details. We glorify the Lord Jesus Christ by showing what he really has done to us, what he has made of us, and, in particular, what he came into the world to do. So, why did he come into the world? If you simply read the gospels you will find that they answer the question immediately: 'The Son of man is come to seek and to save that which was lost' (Lk 19:10). 'The Son of man came not to be ministered unto, but to minister, and to give his life a ransom for many' (Mt 20:28). 'I am come that they might have life, and that they might have it more abundantly' (Jn 10:10). 'I am the light of the world: he that followeth me shall not walk in darkness, but shall have the light of life' (Jn 8:12). 'I am not come to call the righteous but sinners to repentance' (Mt 9:13). Those are his statements, and there are many others, and the questions, therefore, which we all have to put to ourselves are these: are we demonstrating these things? Are we today, in our lives, by being what we are, proving that the Son of God has succeeded in his mission? Are we living epistles, read of all men, commending him, testifying to him and the power of his grace? That, the New Testament tells us, is what is meant by being a Christian. The Christian is not merely a man who holds certain high ideals and views with regard to various questions and problems – so many think that. No, a Christian is specifically a man who is a living proof that the Son of God succeeded in his mission in this life: 'I am glorified in them.'

We must, therefore, think this through, and in order to help us in this, let us remind ourselves of some other statements which are made with respect to him. The apostle Paul, in writing to the Corinthians, describes him as 'the power of God, and the wisdom of God' in this matter of salvation: 'Unto the Jews a stumblingblock, and unto the Greeks foolishness; but unto them which are called … Christ the power of God, and the wisdom of God' (1 Cor 1:23-24). Again, he says that, to the saved, the Lord Jesus Christ has been made wisdom, and righteousness, and sanctification, and redemption (v. 30); he is the all and in all. Those are the descriptions that are given of him, and so we glorify him by proving that all those statements are nothing but the literal truth. And thereby we establish the fact that we are Christian. In other words, do we individually as Christians prove that Christ and his gospel are indeed the power of God unto salvation? As we have seen, if we can be explained in terms of temperament, or tradition, or backbone, or solely in terms of will-power and our own moral striving and effort – if we can be explained in any way apart from Christ, then, as I understand a text like this, we are just not Christian. A Christian is someone who is all along glorifying Christ, Christ is the only explanation of what he or she is.

How, then, do we prove that he is indeed the wisdom and the power of God? We do so, he has repeated so often in his prayer, by showing that we have been separated from the world and that we are spiritually alive. For the world is not spiritually alive, it is dead, dead in its trespasses and sins, not interested in spiritual things and bored by them. The world regards the Bible as the most boring book under the heavens, and prayer it just cannot understand. To listen to addresses or sermons is the height of tedium, says the world – why? It is because it has not a spiritual faculty. There is a complete deadness and absence of something vital, there is no life. But Christ quickens us to life and power, and thereby he proves that he is the power of God unto salvation.

Another way in which it is often put in the Scriptures is that we have been translated from the power of darkness into the kingdom of God's dear Son. We are all born as the children of wrath and into the kingdom of the devil; we are dupes of Satan and under his dominion. But when a man becomes a Christian, a certain power lays hold upon him and it takes him and transfers him to another kingdom. It is a power; it is not a theory, or a philosophy, it is not a mere point of view. No, says Paul, 'I am not ashamed of the gospel of Christ: for it is the power of God unto salvation' (Rom 1:16) – it translates us, moves us from one position to another. In other words, the Christian is a man to whom something has happened. The power of God has laid hold upon him. That is the first thing that must be true about him, and, therefore, if we would know for certain whether we are Christian or not, and whether we are glorifying Christ or not, that is obviously the first test – are we a living proof and example that the tremendous power of the Son of God has literally taken hold of us and transferred us into the kingdom of God's dear Son? Are we manifesting this power? Have we life and is this dynamic of God and of his Son evident and manifest in us?

But let us look at this in a little more detail. Christ, 'of God is made unto us wisdom, and righteousness, and sanctification, and redemption'. Now that, says Paul in 1 Corinthians 1:31, is God's way of solving the problem of man and the world. The Greek philosophers had done their best, but no, the world by its wisdom knew not God, and they did not succeed. *This* is God's way of doing it, says Paul: Christ and him crucified is God's wisdom. Christ is made unto us redemption and it is a complete redemption – wisdom, righteousness, sanctification and finally redemption – and the Christian glorifies Christ by proving that this is true. One reason for the coming of the Lord Jesus Christ into the world was that mankind was ignorant of God, there was an estrangement between man and God. And the world today still does not know God, and by its wisdom cannot find him. So, in a sense, the first task of the Lord was to bring us to this knowledge of God. As he has already been saying in his prayer, he has come to give 'eternal life to as many as thou hast given him. And this is life eternal, that they might know thee the only true God, and Jesus Christ, whom thou hast sent'.

We are dealing with practical things here, so I simply have to ask a series of questions. Do you *know* God? Is he real to you or is he just a philosophy? Is he but a category of thought, or merely a kind of concept that you play with in working out your system of belief? Or is he the almighty God, real to you – do you really know him? I, says Christ to his Father, am glorified in them. I have come into the world in order to make you known to them and they are the people who prove that I have succeeded, for they know me.

So the first way by which I, in practice, glorify the Lord Jesus Christ is that I can testify that I know God. I do not, therefore, go down on my knees with the poet and say,

> I thank whatever gods may be
> For my unconquerable soul
> *W.E. Henley*

Not at all! I go on my knees and I pray to one whom I know as my Father, and I know him as my Father because Christ came, and I glorify him in that way. I prove that he has indeed established this righteousness.

But obviously that is not enough. Before I can come to that knowledge, he must have reconciled me to the Father. There is an estrangement between God and man, and that is because of sin: 'Your iniquities have separated between you and your God, and your sins have hid his face from you ...' says the prophet Isaiah (59:2) and the Lord Jesus Christ came into the world to deal with this problem of sin, to remove it, and to get rid of the barrier. He came to make peace between God and man, and no peace is possible between us until the barrier of sin has been removed. He came, as we have seen, to 'give his life a ransom for many' (Mt 20:28), so that our sins might be dealt with and be forgiven, that they might be put away once and for ever.

So a Christian is a person who glorifies the Lord Jesus Christ by knowing that his sins are forgiven, and by showing that he is one who has found peace with God. Surely Christ is glorified most of all when a man who is born in sin, who has been a sinner and has, perhaps, committed terrible sins, can nevertheless say, 'I rejoice now in the knowledge that all my sins are forgiven.' He is not glorifying himself by saying that, but Christ. He cannot himself get rid of his sins, he cannot generate peace, he cannot quieten his own conscience, he cannot say he loves God. No, it is Christ and Christ alone who does it all, and the man who says that he knows his sins are forgiven is glorifying the Lord Jesus Christ. But the man who is doubtful whether he is forgiven or not is not glorifying Christ, neither is the man who says, 'I hope my sins are forgiven', nor yet the man who says, 'I am living as good a life as I can in order to atone for my past.' The man who glorifies Christ is the man who can say, 'Therefore being justified by faith, we have peace with God ... and rejoice in hope of the glory of God' (Rom 5:1–2).

Do you *know* that your sins are forgiven? Have you got assurance of salvation? Are you certain of it? For to the extent that you are, you glorify Christ, and to the extent that you are uncertain, you are not glorifying him. What proves that he has done the work he was sent to do is that we have the knowledge of sins forgiven and that we rejoice in it. He came very specially to do this and therefore we glorify him by proving that he really has done it. It sounds a simple question yet it is the profoundest question a man can ever face, so let me ask it again. Are you certain of God? Do you *know* God? Are you happy about your relationship to him? My dear friends, the Son of God not only came from heaven to earth, he went deliberately to the cross and suffered all the ignominy and shame of that cross in order that you and I might be certain, certain without any doubt at all, of our relationship to God as his children.

But let me hasten from righteousness to sanctification. 'He is made unto us wisdom, righteousness, sanctification ...' and sanctification is that which shows and proves that Christ is in us, and that he is working in us and that he is producing a certain effect within us. He said in the previous chapters of John's gospel that he would pray to the Father and 'he shall give you another Comforter, that he may abide with you for ever; even the Spirit of truth; whom the world cannot receive, because it seeth him not, neither knoweth him: but ye know him; for he dwelleth with you, and shall be in you' (Jn 14:16–17). Don't be brokenhearted because I am going, he says. 'It is expedient for you that I go away: for if I go not away, the Comforter will not come unto you; but if I depart, I will send him unto you' (Jn 16:7). He himself is going to come, through the Holy Spirit. He is going to take up his abode in us, he, and the Father also, are going to dwell in us, and he says that he has come to make that possible. So we glorify him by proving that he has done that, and, to put it negatively again, the extent to which we do not prove that, is the extent to which we are not glorifying him.

How, then, does this work out in practice? We can show it in several ways. We prove it by not living in sin. I am not saying that we are sinless and that we are perfect. No, what I am saying is that the Christian does not live in sin, or dwell in it, he does not '*abide in sin*'. That is the great theme of the first epistle of

John, a letter which, as Christians, we can never read too frequently. John says that the Christian does not continue in sin,
he does not abide in it, because he has been taken out of it. He
may fail sometimes, but he does not continue in sin as he did
before. Not only that, he has an increasing awareness of sin in
himself, and of the subtlety and the whole meaning of it, and he
comes to feel, therefore, an increasing hatred of sin. That is
always the effect of the working of the Holy Spirit in us and,
too, it is the typical effect of the indwelling Christ, of the resi-
dence of Christ in a man's life. He becomes more and more sensitive to sin, and increasingly conscious of it, and so he comes to
hate it more and more. The more sensitive we become to sin,
the more we glorify Christ. The more we become aware of the
blackness of our own heart, and the wretchedness of our old,
fallen nature, again, the more we glorify him. The man of the
world is not aware of these things. If you talk to him about the
old nature and the new, he will regard it as something strange,
because Christ is not in him. But the moment Christ comes in
there is a conflict: 'The flesh lusteth against the Spirit, and the
Spirit against the flesh: and these are contrary the one to the
other' (Gal 5:17) – all that is indicative of the presence of Christ
and therefore it glorifies him.

But let me come to the more positive statement: it also means
that there is now a power within us to resist temptation and sin
and to conquer them. Christ conquered the devil. He defeated
and routed him, and if he dwells in us, we should defeat him
too. 'Resist the devil, and he will flee from you,' writes James
(Jas 4:7), and we find Peter saying the same thing: 'Be sober, be
vigilant; because your adversary the devil, as a roaring lion,
walketh about, seeking whom he may devour' (1 Pet 5:8) – and
what do we do about him? – 'Whom resist stedfast in the
faith...' (v.9), and thereby you conquer him. Do we conquer
temptation and sin? We glorify Christ if we do, but if we do not
we are not glorifying him, for if we are still being mastered and
defeated by these things; the suggestion is that he has not done
what he claimed to do.

But let us go on. We manifest his glory by showing the

world an increasing delight in spiritual things. Has the Bible become more and more interesting to you? Do you enjoy it increasingly? Do you like studying it, not in a mechanical sense, but in a spiritual sense? What about prayer, fellowship and communion with God? He came to earth and he went to the cross in order that we might know this only true God, and Jesus Christ whom he sent. He himself spent much time in praying to his Father, so is prayer an increasing delight to us? The more we pray and enjoy it, the more we glorify Christ because we are a living proof of the fact that he succeeded in doing what he came to do. Fellowship with others? 'We know that we have passed from death unto life, because we love the brethren' (1 Jn 3:14). Do we delight in God's people and the things that they talk about, these things of the soul and of the spirit, rather than in others who have no interest in these things? That is another wonderful way of glorifying Christ.

Furthermore, our Lord says in Matthew 5:6, 'Blessed are they which do hunger and thirst after righteousness.' Can we say that we have an increasing hunger and thirst after righteousness, that we desire more and more to be holy, to 'know him, and the power of his resurrection, and the fellowship of his sufferings, being made conformable unto his death' (Phil 3:10)? Do we know something of this spirit that was in Paul and which made him feel like that, and urged him to press forward to that glorious perfection that is in Christ himself? Yes, that sums it all up – a desire to be like him.

Let me also suggest another great question for our consideration. I suppose that, supremely, we glorify Christ by proving that he has given to us the gift of the Holy Spirit. If you read the gospels and the Acts of the Apostles, you will find it constantly reiterated that he came into the world in order that the promise of the Father might be given to us. And the promise of the Father is the coming of the Holy Spirit. Our Lord goes in order that he may send the gift of the Spirit – it is a marvellous thing. So we glorify Christ by showing that we have received the Holy Spirit, that the gift has come to us. And according to the apostle Paul in Galatians 5:22–23, we do that by manifesting the fruit of the Spirit in our ordinary, daily life.

What, then, is the fruit of the Spirit? First of all, Paul tells us, it is *love*. The Christian whose nature is increasingly one of love shows that he has received the Spirit, and he thereby glorifies the Lord Jesus Christ. I am glorified in them, he says, when they show a loving nature and a loving character. Then there is *joy*. I only touch upon joy here because I shall be coming back to it, but the more joyful we are as Christians, the more we glorify Christ. His was a life of joy in spite of all that he endured, and the more joy there is in our lives, the more we glorify him – 'Rejoice in the Lord alway: and again I say, rejoice' (Phil 4:4).

Next comes *peace*, a peace within, a tranquillity, a steadiness of life. A peacemaker is one who radiates peace wherever he is, he is not a busybody, or a person who upsets everything and causes division. Then after love, joy and peace, there is *longsuffering*, being able to bear with people, not irritable, not easily put out, not angular, not offensive, however sorely tried. And then, *gentleness*. It is a very difficult thing in this modern world to be gentle, but, my friends, the more gentle you and I are, and the more gentle we become, the more the Lord Jesus Christ is glorified in us. And the same is true of *goodness*, essential goodness, a good character, and *faith* – here meaning faithfulness. Then comes one of the most remarkable of all – *meekness*. I do not think that the modern world knows anything at all about meekness; we are all of us given to advertising or propaganda. Of course we do it for the sake of getting on, but if we want to glorify Christ and to advertise him, the high road to that is to be meek ourselves. Then lastly there is *temperance*, which is self-control, discipline in our thought, in our actions, in everything.

We could spend much time with everyone of these, but I am trying here to give you a composite picture. The extent to which this marvellous fruit of the Spirit is manifest in our lives is the measure and the extent to which Christ is being glorified in us, because the fruit of the Spirit is nothing but a description of the life and the character of the Lord Jesus Christ himself.

That is the sort of person he was, and he tells us that he came into the world in order to make us like himself. So the more we resemble him, the more we glorify him, and the more we prove that he really has succeeded in doing what he came to do.

But, further, we glorify him in the most remarkable way by our attitude to this world, and to life in this world. Here again we must be like him. The most difficult thing of all, perhaps, in this life is not to be conquered by the world, not to be mastered or governed by it. Most people are defeated by it. They are slaves to the circle in which they move, and to the way in which they are expected to live. But he did not conform. He lived his own life separate from the world; he overcame the world and the Christian is meant to do the same. 'This is the victory that overcometh the world, even our faith' (1 Jn 5:4). So if you and I show in our lives that we have seen through this world with all its tinsel and all its vain and empty pomp and show, if we prove that we are living above it and mastering it, then we are glorifying him and we are like him. And the extent to which we are certain of the blessed hope that is set before us is again the extent to which we glorify him.

It means, therefore, that we are able to endure trials and persecution for his name's sake, in the way he did himself. I suppose the people above all others in the long history of the church who have glorified Christ the most, have been the martyrs and the confessors, the men who went to the stake without hesitation, glorifying him, while the world stood and looked on, amazed and astounded. These men were prepared to do it for him – 'There must be something in it,' said the onlooking world, and thereby the martyrs and the confessors glorified Christ. Are we ready to be persecuted? Not by being sent to the stake or even thrown into prison perhaps, but by just observing that when we enter a room people look at one another with a smirk on their faces, or a cruel taunt on their lips? Are we ready to endure it for Christ's sake? The world may know nothing about us, our names may never appear in the newspapers, but if we just take that and endure it, as he did, for his name's sake, he is glorified in us.

And I suppose the last way of all in which we glorify him is by the way in which we die. The old fathers always used to observe very closely the way in which Christian people died. It was, they thought, a marvellous test, and you never read the old biographies without noticing a great emphasis on that. If when we are lying on our death bed we hear the trumpet sounding, if we see him awaiting us, if we see something of the glory that is before us and if we can thank him for everything and just surrender ourselves and our spirits into his blessed hands – Oh what a testimony to him, what a way of glorifying him! He has taken the sting out of death for the Christian. To die is gain, says Paul, it is to be with Christ, which is far better.

There, then, are some of the ways in which we can glorify our blessed Lord and Saviour. There is something glorious in these words, but there is also something pathetic about them. 'I am glorified in them.' Look at the sort of people those disciples were! And yet he was glorified in them and he has been glorified in the countless millions of unknown Christian people throughout the centuries. And to us too in this dark, evil, ugly age is given the privilege of glorifying him today.

May I suggest a practical rule for you as I close. I know of no better way of starting my day than by saying to myself every morning: 'I am one of the people in the world today through whom Christ is to be glorified. I am not here for myself, or for anything I want to do, the main thing for me this day is that Christ should be glorified in me.' Start your day by saying that to yourself, and when you are praying to God remind yourself of what you are and what he expects. Remind yourself of it several times during the day, recollect now and again, take a second just to say to yourself, 'I am the one through whom Christ is to be glorified and praised.' And then the last thing at night before you go to sleep ask yourself this question: has Christ been glorified in my life today? Have I manifested the fruit of the Spirit? Have I been showing love, joy, peace, longsuffering, gentleness, goodness, meekness, faith and temperance? – Or have I lost my temper, have I been irritable, have I upset people?

Have I been a storm centre or have I taken with me the peace of Christ and of God? Have I, by being what I have been this day, made people look towards him with a longing to know him and to be like him?

'I am glorified in them.'

9

True Joy

And now I come to thee; and these things I speak in the world, that they might have my joy fulfilled in themselves (v. 15).

We have been considering together the ways in which, as Christians, we manifest our Lord's glory, and we have reminded ourselves of our tremendous responsibility as we realize that we, and we alone, are the people through whom the Lord Jesus Christ is glorified in this world of time.

Now that was the second reason for our Lord's prayer – the first reason, you remember, was because of who and what we are – and here we come to the third reason, which he puts quite plainly in verse 13. He says, in effect, 'I am praying all these things audibly in their presence because I am anxious that they might have my joy fulfilled in themselves.' He is anxious that this joy that he himself had experienced should also be fully experienced by these his followers. There is, therefore, a very definite logical sequence in the arrangement of these matters. In dealing earlier with the ways in which the Lord Jesus Christ is glorified in us, we spoke of the fruit of the Spirit, which is love, joy, peace, and so on. At that point, in dealing briefly with joy, I said that I would not go into it in detail, because we would be returning to it, and this is where we must do that. And what we see here is that one of the ways in which we, as Christians, can glorify Christ in this life and world, is by being filled with this spirit of joy and of rejoicing. This is a fruit of the Spirit which

106

our Lord singles out in particular in this prayer to the Father on
behalf of his followers. And so we glorify him in a very special
way by being partakers of this his own joy.

Obviously, therefore, this is an important subject. Our Lord
would not have singled it out like this and given it a special place
and emphasis unless it was something of vital concern. So
clearly we must start our consideration of it by reminding ourselves again of what a wonderful display this is of our Lord's
care and solicitude for his own people. How anxious he is that
their welfare should be catered for! He is going to leave them,
he is going back to the Father, but he does not lose interest in
them for that reason. In a sense he is still more interested in
them, and though he is going to face the shame and the agony
of the cross, what is uppermost in his mind is the condition and
future of these disciples of his, whom he is leaving behind.

But there is more than that – indeed it is something which is
of even more vital concern. All that we have been saying is
something to rejoice in, but there is a bigger, deeper lesson here.
This whole subject of joy is one which is prominent in the New
Testament, and, therefore, it must be of primary importance to
Christian people. We can see in John 16 how our Lord constantly referred to it, and if you go through the four gospels and
look for it, you will find that he was always emphasizing it. And
if you read the epistles you will find the subject of joy there, in
perhaps a still more striking manner, for some of them are
almost exclusively devoted to it. It is a great theme, for instance,
of the epistle to the Philippians. Paul's concern there is that
Christian people should experience this joy – 'Rejoice in the
Lord alway: and again I say, Rejoice' (4:4). It was his burning
desire for all Christian people. And then, what, after all, is the
purpose of the book of Revelation except that God's people
should be taught how truly to be filled with joy and to rejoice?
John himself in his first epistle very specifically says, 'These
things write I unto you that your joy might be full' (1:14). He
was an old man realizing that he was at the end of his journey
and thinking of the Christian people he was leaving behind in
this difficult world. So he wrote his letter to them in order that

their joy might be full. It is, I say, one of the outstanding themes
of the entire New Testament, and so it behoves us to be very
clear in our minds about it.

There are certain principles that seem to me to stand out very
clearly. The first is that we are not only saved for eternity. The
gospel of Jesus Christ, of course, is primarily something that
does safeguard our eternal destiny. Its fundamental purpose is
to reconcile us to God and to see that we are saved in that final
and eternal sense. It puts us right once and for all and into a right
standing in the presence of God. It reconciles us to God, and
establishes definitely in our experience that we are his children.
It takes from us the fear of death, of the grave, and of judgement, and it assures us that our eternity and our eternal destiny
is safe and secure. But – and this is what is emphasized in this
particular verse – we are not only saved for eternity. It is a very
false and incomplete view of Christian salvation that postpones
its blessings to the realm that lies beyond this present life and
beyond the grave.

This sounds so obvious that it is almost foolish to emphasize
it, and yet if you go into the history of the church you will find
that very often, and sometimes for a very long period, Christian
people, by the subtlety of Satan, have been entirely robbed of
this particular aspect. This has very often been a result of our
reaction – a healthy and right reaction – against worldliness.
Christian people have realized that because they are not of the
world they should separate themselves from everything that
belongs to it. They interpret that as meaning that while they are
in this life they are – to use that line of Milton's – 'To scorn
delights, and live laborious days'. So they have thought of the
Christian as someone who is melancholic, someone who is
never going to experience any happiness or joy in a sinful world
like this, but who really does look forward to a great joy of
unmixed bliss in the land that lies beyond the present and the
seen. Thus they seem to rob themselves entirely of any benefits
or blessings from salvation in this present life. Now that is tragically and pathetically wrong. The blessings of Christianity are
to be enjoyed in this world as well as in the world to come.

There are different aspects, of course, of salvation, but we must never so emphasize the future as to derogate from the present, neither must we in turn emphasize the present and detract from the future. There are blessings to be enjoyed here and now and our Lord emphasized that very clearly in this verse.

But then I draw a second deduction, which is that one of the particular blessings which the Christian is meant to enjoy in the present life is this experience of joy. Our Lord says that he prays in order that his joy might be 'fulfilled in themselves'. We see that in John 16 when he exhorts us to pray: 'Hitherto have ye asked nothing in my name: ask, and ye shall receive, that your joy may be full' (v. 24). The Christian is meant to be a joyful person, one who is meant to experience the joy of salvation. There is no question about that; it is something which is taught everywhere in the New Testament, and so it is our duty as Christians to have this joy, and to be filled with it. And we must give ourselves neither rest nor peace until we have it.

But there are many obstacles to that, and many things which hinder the Christian from having it. There are certain people, I know, who so react against the false and carnal sort of joy, that they rob themselves of the true joy. But the opposite of carnal and fleshly joy is not to be miserable. It is to have the true joy, the joy of the Lord Jesus Christ himself. And in the light of all these exhortations from him and from the apostles we must start by realizing that it is our duty to possess and to experience this joy of which our Lord speaks. We have no right not to have it. Indeed, I put it as my third principle that it is clearly dishonouring to the Lord Jesus Christ, and to the work he has done, not to have this joy. The teaching seems to be that he came into this world in order that we might have it. Take, for instance, the words at the end of chapter 16: 'These things I have spoken unto you, that in me ye might have peace' (v.33). That verse couples peace and joy together: 'In the world ye shall have tribulation: but be of good cheer; I have overcome the world.' And because he has overcome the world, we are meant to have this joy and to experience it; we are meant to be Christian people who rejoice.

This links very naturally with the previous subject of glorifying him – a miserable Christian does not and obviously cannot glorify the Lord Jesus Christ. Everybody else is miserable, the world makes people so. But if the Lord Jesus Christ has done what he claims to have done, and has come to suffer all that he suffered in this world, to the end that his people might be made different, they are obviously to be a joyful people. He has done all that in order to make it possible for us, and so our failure to be joyful in our lives is to detract from his glory and to cast queries upon his wonderful work. It thus behoves us as Christian people to realize that it is our duty to be joyful. This is often put to us in the New Testament as an injunction. We are commanded to rejoice and if you are commanded to do something, it means that you *must* do it. Now that, obviously, is going to raise a question in our minds as to the nature of this joy. People say that it is no use going to a miserable man and telling him to cheer up. But there is a sense in which you can do that – not directly, but indirectly – and it will result in joy. This is what we must consider together. 'Rejoice in the Lord alway: and again I say, Rejoice' – that is what we are meant to do, and we are meant to be joyful, not only for our own sakes, but still more for his.

So that leads us to the vital question – what is this joy, and what do we know about it? We will content ourselves, for the moment, with just looking at what our Lord himself tells us in this particular verse. The first thing is that it is *his* joy. 'These things I speak in the world, that they might have *my* joy fulfilled in themselves.' Now this is most important because it means that it is not the kind of joy that some people sometimes seem to think it is. It is the kind of joy that he himself possessed and therefore we can say of necessity that it was not carnal or fleshly, it was never boisterous.

I emphasize those negatives because it is always essential to point out that in a matter like this there are two extremes that must always be avoided. I have already mentioned one of them, that of being so anxious to avoid the carnal as to become almost melancholic, but we must also avoid this other extreme. There are certain people – and they have been very much in evidence

I should think for the last fifty years or so – who, having realized quite rightly that a Christian is meant to have joy, have been so anxious to manifest the fact that though they are Christian they are still joyful, that they assume a liveliness which is certainly not the joy of the Lord Jesus Christ. They are a kind of boisterous Christian, but our Lord was never boisterous. Our Lord's joy was a holy joy. Yes – let us not hesitate to say it – it was a serious joy. He was a man of sorrows and acquainted with grief and yet joyful.

The same thing is obviously true of the apostle Paul. He says of himself that he knows this joy and rejoices, and yet he also says that 'in this tabernacle do we groan, being burdened' (2 Cor 5:4). You just cannot think of Paul as a kind of 'hail fellow well met' man, it is inconceivable. Yet no man had a greater joy. He talked in the terms of our Lord himself, and that is the joy that you and I should have. It is not a kind of joy that you put on as a cloak, nor is it a kind of mask that you put on to impress people with how happy and joyful you are. To start with, that does not mislead anybody except the truly superficial, but in any case it is false. True joy is not something that is assumed, it is, rather, an experience down in the depths of one's being. It is not, therefore, something you try to produce, but something that you are, which manifests itself in your life because you are what you are. There is nothing, it seems to me, that is so irritating as the kind of person who is obviously trying to give the impression that he is happy and joyful because he is a Christian, there is nothing that tends to make some of us more miserable; but that is a wrong sort of joy. The first principle, then, is that it is a particular type of joy. It is his joy, and it is the very antithesis of the carnal and fleshly, which is assumed and affected and acted.

Secondly, it is exactly the joy that our Lord himself knew. You cannot go through the gospels and look at the portrayal of our Lord which is contained therein, without seeing this remarkable theme running right through. In spite of all he had to endure and suffer, he spoke constantly of this joy. There is no more striking illustration of this than that which we find at the end of chapter 16. The disciples, at long last, thought that they had seen and understood, but he turned to them and said – and if I could paint I should like to paint the expression of his face when he said it – 'Do ye now believe? Behold, the hour cometh, yea, is now come, that ye shall be scattered, every man to his own, and shall leave me alone' – then – 'and yet I am not alone, because the Father is with me' (Jn 16:31–32). That is joy, that is the joy which he possessed, it was always a part of his life and experience. And that is the joy which we are meant to have, a joy that can face the cross, yes, and the weakness and the apparent desertion, of those whom we trusted, and on whom we relied – 'Who for the joy that was set before him endured the cross, despising the shame…' (Heb 12:2).

Or, again, you can look at it as the joy that comes entirely and exclusively from him. He is its source, so it is a joy that is impossible apart from him, because it derives and emanates from him. It is a joy that he gives to his own people. Put in another way, it is a part of this wonderful fruit that the Holy Spirit produces in us, so in no sense is it self-generated. We do not produce it, it is his joy which is thus realized by us and manifested through us – that is our first principle.

The second thing he tells us about it is that it is a joy that is entirely above and independent of the world and of circumstances and it is in no way produced by them. That, as we have just seen, is the thing that stands out so marvellously in the life of the Lord himself and that is what strikes you as you read through the gospels. He was in the world yet he was not of it, he was independent of it. He walked through the middle of the storm quite unaffected by it, for he had peace within. It is said that in the middle of a hurricane, or a tornado, there is always a central spot which is quite peaceful, and our Lord was always there. Whatever might be happening around and about him, he had this central point of peace and joy. Again, we see this clearly in the great verse in Hebrews 12: 'Who for the joy that was set before him endured the cross, despising the shame.' He went through it all, for there was that about him which made him quite impervious to these things and they could not get at him. It was a kind of garrison, or, as Paul puts it in connection with peace, 'The peace of God, which passeth all understanding, shall keep [garrison] your hearts and minds' (Phil 4:7), shall surround them, or shall so protect them that nothing can penetrate.

Our Lord was like that; he was kept by this marvellous joy so that nothing could touch or affect him. After all, there is very little value in a joy which does not make us capable of that. If our joy is dependent upon what is happening to us and the world around us, or on what is happening to us physically, then we are not different from the world. The world knows what it is to have a kind of joy when everything goes well, but the tragedy about worldly joy is that it is entirely dependent upon circumstances. We all know that perfectly well in our own experience, and we see it so constantly in others. I know of nothing which is quite so sad in this world as to see a life that has seemed so happy suddenly shattered because of something that happens, such as the death of a loved one, or some disappointment or accident. The joy which is thus dependent upon circumstances outside ourselves or our own condition is not his joy. The glory of this joy of which he speaks is that it is absolutely independent of circumstances. He could face the cross and rejoice, and his prayer to the Father is that this joy might be fulfilled in us.

We must remember, too, the context of this verse. He goes on to say in verses 14–16, 'I have given them thy word; and the world hath hated them, because they are not of the world, even as I am not of the world. I pray not that thou shouldest take them out of the world, but that thou shouldest keep them from the evil. They are not of the world, even as I am not of the world.' That is the promise. He was going to leave them all. They had been dependent on him – for three years they had been hanging on his every word, and the result was that when he began to tell them he was going away, sorrow filled their hearts. And so he started off – we read at the beginning of the fourteenth chapter – by saying, 'Let not your heart be troubled: ye believe in God, believe also in me …' He tried to comfort them. He said, in effect, 'You are depending too much on my physical presence. I am going to leave you.' But not only that, he was going to leave them in a world full of hate, in a world that hated them, in a world that would be antagonistic to them, in a world that would try to kill them and exterminate them, as a body. He was going to leave them in such a world, and yet his prayer was, 'That they might have my joy fulfilled in them.' In other words, his prayer was that though the world, the flesh, the devil and all hell would be let loose against them and would be violently opposed to them, yet they – like himself, for the joy that was set before them, the joy that they had already experienced – might be more than conquerors. That is the great New Testament theme. Read Romans 8, verses 35–37, where Paul, after he had given his tremendous list of all the things that were happening to them, could write, 'Nay, in all these things we are more than conquerors through him that loved us.' That is the true joy. It is a joy, therefore, that is entirely above circumstances and accident and chance; it is independent of them all even as his was.

And the next principle is the discovery of what it is that makes this joy possible. I can imagine someone saying, 'I would give the whole world if I could have this joy. I recognize that you are right when you say it is the New Testament teaching, and that it is my duty to be like that, but how does one get it?'

Fortunately our Lord answers the question here. He says, 'These things I speak in the world; [in order] that they might have my joy fulfilled in themselves', and that leads us to see exactly how we can obtain this joy. One part of this joy is our certain knowledge that he is praying for us. He not only prayed for the disciples, he prayed audibly, in order that they might hear and know, and what he did there he will do for us now. Therefore the great thing is to know that the Lord Jesus Christ is interceding on our behalf, he is still praying.

And that, in turn, leads us to realize his love towards us. I suppose there is nothing that so tends to rob us of our joy as our realization that we do not love him as we ought, because when we realize this, we become unhappy and miserable. I will tell you the best antidote to that: when you realize your love is weak and faint and poor and unworthy, stop thinking about your love, and realize that in spite of its poverty, he loves you. He has said, 'As the Father hath loved me, so have I loved you' (Jn

15:9). If I did not believe that, then I would be of all men most wretched and miserable, for the whole essence of the Christian salvation is to know that in spite of what I have been and what I am, he loves me. Start with that, and I think he will begin to make you love him, but if you are always looking at your own love and trying to increase that, you will be miserable. Think of his love to you; he has given evidence of it, so accept the evidence and act upon it.

But it also makes us know the Father's love. Our Lord has said it here, in verse 6: 'thine they were' – he reminds us that we belong to God, that we are God's people, the special object of his concern. Or let me put it still more specifically in this way. What are 'these things' to which our Lord refers? They are this great doctrine that he has been enunciating, which is that God has his people, that before the foundation of the world God had his people, his marked people, and that he gave them to Christ – we have already dealt with this in detail: 'I have manifested thy name unto the men which thou gavest me out of the world: thine they were, and thou gavest them me' (v.6). To know the Lord's joy is to realize that, and to realize, furthermore, that the Lord Jesus Christ came into the world for us, that he came in order to prepare us for God, and to deliver us from the guilt of our sin. He has done it all. He has borne the guilt and the punishment and the law is satisfied. It has nothing against us any more, for, 'There is therefore now no condemnation to them which are in Christ Jesus' (Rom 8.1). As the hymn puts it, 'The terrors of law and of God, With me can have nothing to do' (Augustus Montague Toplady). I know that, and he has reminded me of it, so how can I fail to be joyful if I believe what he says?

Then what more can we say about these things? Well, he has given me his own nature. He has made me a child of God. He gives me the blessed assurance that, 'If, when we were enemies, we were reconciled to God by the death of his Son, much more, being reconciled, we shall be saved by his life' (Rom 5:10). He has shown us so plainly and clearly that our salvation depends entirely upon him, and not upon ourselves at all. He has told us that no man shall be able to pluck us out of his hands, that we are indeed safe and secure, and that nothing and no one shall be able to separate us from the love of God which is in Christ Jesus our Lord. It is people who believe things like that, who know what this joy is. Go back and read the history of the church, read the lives of the saints, and you will find that the people who have been the most joyful have always been the people who have been most assured and certain of their salvation.

And then another source of joy is that we can realize, as he did, the joy that is set before us. Whatever this world may be doing to us, if we know of this inheritance that is prepared for us we cannot but be happy. 'Let not your heart be troubled: ye believe in God, believe also in me. In my Father's house are many mansions: if it were not so, I would have told you. I go to prepare a place for you. And if I go and prepare a place for you, I will come again, and receive you unto myself; that where I am, there ye may be also' (Jn 14:1–3). If you believe that, your heart cannot but rejoice. So he speaks 'these things' in the world that we may hear them, and this is the source of joy.

And all that leads in turn to fellowship with the Father, to a life lived with God. John has put that perfectly, once and for ever, in 1 John 1:3–4, 'That which we have seen and heard declare we unto you, that ye also may have fellowship with us: and truly our fellowship is with the Father, and with his Son Jesus Christ. And these things write we unto you, that your joy may be full.' That is the ultimate source of joy, that, realizing the truth as it is in Christ, we are brought into fellowship with the Father. And so, as we walk with him in fellowship we must be joyful. Anything less is impossible, and as our Lord experienced it, so shall we experience it.

So let me end this study with a few practical suggestions. How, then, in practice do we have this joy? The first thing is to avoid concentrating on our own feelings. There are many Christian people who spend the whole of their lives looking at their own feelings and always taking their own spiritual pulse, their own spiritual temperature. Of course, they never find it satisfactory, and because of that they are miserable and unhappy, moaning and groaning. Now that is wrong. First and foremost we must avoid concentrating on our own feelings. We must learn to concentrate positively on 'these things'. In other words, the secret of joy is the practice of meditation – that is the way to have this joy of the Lord. We must meditate upon him, upon what he is, what he has done, his love to us and upon God's care for us who are his people.

This is what I meant earlier when I said we could only produce this joy indirectly. It is not something I assume in order to give the impression that I am a wonderfully happy man, and then go back to being bored and miserable in my own home. No, it is not that, it is something that results from meditation and contemplation upon 'these things', these precious, wonderful things. And I have no hesitation in saying that there is such a marked absence of true Christian joy in the church today because there is so little meditation. Do not misunderstand me. We all constantly exhort one another to have our 'quiet time', which generally means reading Scripture and prayer. It is perfectly right, but if you stop at that, you will probably not have this joy – having read and having prayed, then meditate. Think on these things, set your affection on them, hold yourself before them and bring them to your mind many times during the day. The sum of joy is simple meditation, contemplation, on these things, making time to dwell upon them, putting other things out of the way and spending your time with them. For the more we know 'these things' and dwell with them and live with them, and seek the face of God, the greater will be our joy.

And obviously – this almost goes without saying – we must avoid everything that tends to break our fellowship with God. The moment that is broken we become miserable. We cannot help it; whether we want to or not, our conscience will see to that. It will accuse us, and condemn anything that breaks our fellowship with God and his Son. The joy of the world always drives out the other joy, as does any dependence on the world, so we must avoid sin in every shape and form. Let us stop looking to the world, even at its best, for true joy, and for true happiness. But above all, we must look at 'these things' that he speaks of, these truths that he unfolded. Let us meditate upon them, contemplate them, dwell upon them, revel in them and I will guarantee that as we do so, either in our own personal meditation or in reading books about them, we will find ourselves experiencing a joy such as we have never known before. It is inevitable, it follows as the night the day.

'These things speak I in the world, that they might have my joy fulfilled in themselves.' What a wonderful thing that it is possible for us to live in this world, in a measure, even as the blessed Son of God lived, and that as we do so he is glorified in us.

10

Kept and Guarded but ...

And now I am no more in the world, but these are in the world, and I come to thee. Holy Father, keep through thine own name those whom thou hast given me, that they may be one, as we are. While I was with them in the world, I kept them in thy name: those that thou gavest me I have kept, and none of them is lost, but the son of perdition; that the scripture might be fulfilled.... I pray not that thou shouldest take them out of the world, but that thou shouldest keep them from the evil (vv. 11–12, 15).

We have been considering our Lord's main reasons for praying for his disciples, and now we come to his petitions on their behalf, and the first petition is the one which is recorded in verses 11, 12 and 15. It is his great petition that God may keep them and especially that he may keep them in his name. Now this first petition follows very naturally from all that we have been considering hitherto. His desire is that they may be kept continuously in the future, in the condition in which he kept them while he was with them. And he prays that in the light of who they are and what they are, and because of what they are meant to do and the circumstances in which they are placed.

We cannot begin to consider this in detail without again reminding ourselves, with grateful and thankful hearts, of this further expression of our Lord's wonderful concern for his people. We can be quite sure that if we but realized his concern for us, most of our problems would immediately be solved. It

119

is because we forget this and because we fail to realize his love for us, that we tend to become anxious and worried and troubled. It does seem to me, increasingly, that a truly happy and joyful Christian life first begins with just this realization that his concern for us and about us is altogether greater than any concern we may have for ourselves and our well-being, and for our witness and our testimony for him.

Our Lord's great prayer is that God may keep them and keep them in rather a special way. Now there is no doubt but that in this particular instance the translation in the Revised Version is altogether better, and more accurate, than that of the Authorized. The right translation of these verses is undoubtedly as follows: 'Holy Father, keep them in thy name which thou hast given me ... While I was with them, I kept them in thy name which thou hast given me: and I guarded them, and not one of them perished, but the son of perdition ...' (vv 11–12, RV). In other words, the prayer is that he may keep them in his name.[1] The Authorized Version is somewhat misleading here because it says, 'Holy Father, keep through thine own name those whom thou hast given me', when it should really be: '... in thy name which thou hast given me'. We have already seen that God had given him the people, and that has been repeated several times; what our Lord is referring to here is the fact that this particular name of God has been given to him. And he says the same thing in the twelfth verse: '... I kept them in thy name which thou hast given me.' So that, clearly, the petition is that God would keep these, his people, in that name which God had given to him.

In a sense, we have already seen that, in verse 6, where he says, 'I have manifested thy name unto the men which thou gavest me out of the world.' This is the mystic secret, if I may

---

[1] The New International Version has, 'Holy Father, protect them by the power of your name – the name you gave me – so that they may be one as we are one. While I was with them, I protected them and kept them safe by that name you gave me.' (Ed.)

so put it, which the Christian possesses, and it is something which nobody else understands. The Father, when he sent his Son into this world, sent him to declare his name, God's name, and the name, as we have seen, is the peculiar revelation of the person and character of God. This is a name which is only given to those who believe in the Lord Jesus Christ, but the moment we believe, we know God in terms of this, as yet unrevealed to us, secret name. We find this very frequently in the Scriptures. For instance, we are told in Revelation 3 that a name is given to the saints, to God's people, which nobody else knows. It means that the Christian has an understanding of God, and a knowledge of God, which nobody else has. And our Lord's prayer is that these Christians may be kept in that knowledge and in that understanding. It is all summed up by the name – that they may continue to know and to understand through their relationship to God, what God is to them and what they are to God. That is the meaning of this prayer, that they may be kept in the name which God has given them, the name of God himself which the Lord has come to reveal, the special revelation of God which is to be found only in and through our blessed Lord and Saviour Jesus Christ. And that, therefore, is his petition for Christian people now, that we may ever be kept in the full realization of our relationship to God.

But before we can come to consider that in its detail and in its context, we must here, of necessity, notice first of all the claim which our Lord couples with the petition. Not only does he present this petition to his Father, he also adds this: 'While I was with them in the world, I kept them in thy name, which thou hast given me, and none of them is lost but the son of perdition that the Scripture might be fulfilled.'

Obviously we have to deal with this and to define it, not merely because we must do so out of intellectual honesty, nor because we must not omit anything when we are working in detail like this through a passage of Scripture. No, we must look at this because it does contain very high and important and serious doctrine.

First of all, then, let us look at our Lord's claims. He claims two things, 'While I was with them in the world,' he says, 'I *kept* them in thy name which thou hast given me: and I *guarded* them' (RV). Again we must notice the superiority of the Revised Version here, because it brings out the difference between the two words which our Lord uses. 'Keeping' is a more comprehensive word than 'guarding', and the idea behind the word can perhaps best be illustrated by a shepherd's care for his sheep. It is the business of the shepherd to 'keep' the sheep. That means that he always keeps his eye on them. He watches them, supervising them the whole time and taking care of them in the fields so that none stray away or get lost. When they have to be moved he sees to it that they are not driven too quickly, and he always makes sure that they are fed at the right time. Constant care, that is the meaning of the word 'keep'. Now the word 'guard' is a lesser term. To guard means simply to protect against attacks, so you see this covers a more restricted area than the other. Guarding means just that one thing – there are enemies around, and it is the business of the shepherd to protect the flock against them.

But we should thank God for both these terms. They tell us that our Lord does not merely guard us, he also keeps us. He is not only concerned about the attacks on us by the world, and by the evil one, but more than that, he is constantly keeping us, watching over us. He is concerned about our welfare and our well-being positively as well as negatively. He not only prevents attacks, he sees to it that we are always in the right position and in the right place and given the right things. He has this great concern, this oversight. The apostle Peter says, 'Ye were as sheep going astray; but are now returned unto *the Shepherd and Bishop of your souls*' (1 Pet 2:25) – that is what our Lord is to us, the one who looks after all our interests in every way. In these verses his claim is that he has kept them and guarded them, but now he says he is going to leave them, and so he prays to God to keep them and to guard them as he had done.

How, then, and when did our Lord keep and guard them? The gospels, of course, are full of answers to that question, I merely note them. In the first place he had done so by teaching them – in a sense that was the purpose of his teaching, to instruct them in their relationship to God, and in the nature of the Christian life. That is why he preached the Sermon on the Mount, and gave them the Beatitudes, so that they might know the kind of people they were meant to be. All his teaching is designed to do this. He taught them about the world, and its subtlety, about sin, about the flesh and about the devil, for it was only as they were forewarned, that they could be forearmed. So his teaching was a very vital part of his keeping of them.

But not only that. It is remarkable as you go through the gospels to notice the amount of time he spent in warning his followers. There is nothing further removed from the gospels than many of the false cults which say, 'You believe this and all will be well with you.' The gospel does not do that. Our Lord had solemn warnings for these people, and he constantly prepared them for difficulties and dangers. In a sense, they were far too elated; he was almost alarmed at their lack of understanding, and so he warned them. On one occasion they had been out preaching and they had come back so jubilant because, they said, 'Even the devils are subject unto us.' But he said to them, '... in this rejoice not, that the spirits are subject unto you; but rather rejoice, because your names are written in heaven' (Lk 10:17, 20). He knew the things they were going to find, so he warned them, and that is another way of keeping them.

He also keeps them by rebuking them at times, by chastising them. In their lack of understanding they tended to do things which were bad for them and bad for the kingdom, so our Lord rebuked them. 'Whom the Lord loveth he chasteneth' (Heb 12:6) and that is the business of chastening: to keep us, to keep us from straying and from wandering, to keep us from things that are harmful to us. And so in his love he keeps us by rebuking us and by chastening us. But above all, our Lord kept them and guarded them by actual manifestations of his power. He frequently stood between them and the attacks and assaults of the world and the flesh and the devil. That becomes clear quite often. Take, for instance, his words to Peter: 'Simon, Simon, behold, Satan hath desired to have you, that he may sift you as wheat: but I have prayed for thee, that thy faith fail not' (Lk 22:31–32). He knew that these onslaughts were coming, he anticipated them, and in this way he kept them and guarded them.

Now we must surely raise the question as to why our Lord makes this claim at this point. The answer, clearly, is that it is another statement of his to the effect that he has glorified his Father in everything and that he has failed in nothing. You remember we had it at the very beginning of the prayer. 'Father,' he says, 'the hour is come; glorify thy Son, that thy Son also may glorify thee.' That was his purpose, he was always concerned to glorify the Father. In verse 2 he says, 'As thou hast given him power over all flesh, that he should give eternal life to as many as thou hast given him' – and then, in verse 4 – 'I have glorified thee on the earth.' And one of the ways in which he had glorified the Father was that he had kept these men whom the Father had given him. He had not failed in any single respect or detail.

Here again is something which calls for a word of comment. Read the four gospels again and keep this particular point in your mind. Look at the disciples, look at their frailty, their proneness to sinfulness. There was nothing exceptional about them. They were not learned in any way, but just ordinary men in this extraordinary position. Yet our Lord could claim, and claim rightly and truly, that he had kept them, though they were what they were, and in spite of all the temptations to which they had been exposed. He had kept them in these extraordinary circumstances because his strength was sufficient. They were ignorant, they did not understand him at times and they were bewildered and baffled. Yet in spite of all that we may say about them – the impulsiveness of a Peter or the scepticism of a Thomas – our Lord, by his amazing way of dealing with them, had kept and guarded them. And here, at the end, he is able to say to the Father, I have kept, I have guarded these people whom thou hast given me.

Ah yes, but there is, however, one statement which we have to face – '... and,' says our Lord, 'none of them is lost, but the

son of perdition; that the scripture might be fulfilled.' Now this
is something which is truly remarkable. Here, I would remind
you again, is our Lord just under the shadow of the cross, praying to the Father, and in this prayer he mentions the case of
Judas. Why does he do that? As we seek to answer that question,
I think that once more I can show you that this is a very important doctrine for us. First of all, we must notice here that he says
but – 'but the son of perdition' – and not *except*. These two
words always confuse the exegesis of this verse. Our Lord is
saying here that though Judas is one of the twelve, he is not one
of those who has been given to the Son by the Father. Judas is
not a kind of exception among the apostles, he is in a category
apart. He does not really belong to the same group, he is an odd
man out: he is in the group but has never been of it. If our Lord
had said, 'I have kept them all except Judas', the implication
would have been that he had failed to keep one of them. But
when he says, 'I have kept them all *but* the son of perdition', he
is simply saying, Now of these men who have been accom-
panying me I have kept those whom thou hast given me, but
there is one other who has been in the company, the son of perdition, and that is Judas.

Let me say why it is important for us to put it in that form.
We are constantly told in the Scriptures themselves that Judas
was not really one of the true company. Judas was never born
again, and never became a Christian even though he belonged
to the company of the twelve. Let me remind you of John 6:68–
70. When Peter makes his great confession: 'Lord, to whom
shall we go? thou hast the words of eternal life. And we believe
and are sure that thou art that Christ, the Son of the living God,'
our Lord turns to them and says, 'Have not I chosen you twelve,
and one of you is a devil?' And in verse 71 we read: 'He spake
of Judas Iscariot ... for he it was that should betray him, being
one of the twelve.'

So, then, let us return to our question – why does our Lord
mention that at this point in his most tender prayer? The first
answer is one which I have already given – he is praying in an
audible manner, and the disciples are listening to the prayer. He

speaks thus of Judas audibly, in order that he may again claim
in their presence that he has glorified the Father. It is an absolute
claim. He has kept and guarded those whom the Father has
given him: Judas has not been given to him in that way.

Another obvious reason is that he is anxious that these disciples should know beforehand what is going to happen and
what Judas is going to do, lest they be offended when it actually
takes place. Here again is an indication of our Lord's
lovingkindness and his care for his own. Indeed it is a perfect
example of how he keeps them. He knows that Judas is going
to betray him but the others do not. Our Lord spoke of it earlier,
but they did not understand. He now states it again before them,
so that they might know for certain that it is going to happen,
and will not be surprised or dumbfounded at the subtlety of it.

There is a further reason, too. He is anxious to reveal to them
his own deity and to assert that he is the Son of God. He is also
anxious that they should realize his foreknowledge. He knows
exactly what Judas is going to do; he prophesied it earlier, as we
saw, in the sixth chapter. He repeated it in the thirteenth and
now here it is once more. He knows everything. He knows the
end from the beginning, and here he has declared once more that
he is indeed the Son of God. And also, clearly, he says this in
order that he might pay this testimony to Scripture – 'that the
scripture may be fulfilled'. The treachery of Judas is prophesied
in the Scriptures in Psalms 41 and 109. Psalm 109 in particular
gives a detailed description of Judas, and so, as our Lord says
here, the scripture has said it all. He says, in effect, 'It is not only
I, but the scripture, too. The prophets have seen it coming, and
the son of perdition is going to fulfil the prophecy that was
already made long ago.'

That, then, is but the mechanics of this matter, so now let us
apply this great and spiritual message. It seems to me that here
we have, in a terrible picture, the exact difference between
belonging to the world and belonging to the Lord Jesus Christ.
'I pray for them: I pray not for the world.' The difference
between them and the world is the difference between the
eleven and Judas Iscariot. He was not praying for Judas, and he

does not pray for anybody who belongs to the Judas position. So this is the essential difference between being a Christian and not being a Christian, it is all depicted in the alarming picture in this most holy prayer.

Here, then, I suggest, is something by which we ought to examine ourselves, because the lesson at this point is that it is possible for one to belong to the innermost circle and yet to be lost – that is the terrible and terrifying lesson which we must take to ourselves. Mere membership of the church means nothing in and of itself. Judas was one of the twelve and yet he was lost. He was one of those who was sent out with the others and he was one of those who had listened to the most intimate teaching. He was right in the inner circle and yet he was the son of perdition. That is why Scripture constantly exhorts us to examine ourselves. A mechanical position does not guarantee that there is life. There are obviously certain things which characterize this condition of Judas, and we must consider them. The mere fact that I am interested in Christian things does not prove I am a Christian. Why did Judas come among the twelve? For three years he had been with the others and there he was following our Lord and listening to his intimate teaching. There must have been something that attracted him. So we have to realize that we may be attracted to the church, and to the gospel and to Christ himself, and yet not be truly Christian, but sons of perdition.

What are the characteristics of such people? Here are some that seem to be indicated in Scripture. First of all, Judas was dominated by Satan. 'One of you is a devil,' says our Lord in John 6:70, by which he means that this man is entirely, as it were, possessed by the devil, dominated and controlled by him. Then another thing that is very obvious is that he was blinded so that he could not see the truth. As the apostle Paul tells us, 'But if our gospel be hid, it is hid to them that are lost: in whom the god of this world hath blinded the minds of them which believe not, lest the light of the glorious gospel of Christ, who is the image of God, should shine unto them' (2 Cor 4:3–4). Here is a man sitting day by day and listening to the truth from the very Son of God, and yet he never sees it, because he is blinded to it. He hears the words but he does not hear the message. He could probably recite certain words, but he does not know their meaning – he is blind to the truth.

You notice, also, the essential baseness of his character and nature. We are told in John 12:6 '... he was a thief, and had the bag, and bare what was put therein' – he was dishonest. He was in charge of their communal bag and stole from it.[2]   People often have mercenary reasons for belonging to the church; they join for their own selfish ends. Judas was a hypocrite and he pretended to be something he was not. He was treacherous. He was always selfish and self-seeking and the whole tragedy of Judas is that he brought his own interests into the presence of the Son of God himself. It was his avarice that seems to have taken him there. He came to Christ because of certain things he wanted, not because of what Christ had to give, and that is the essential difference between a man who is not a Christian and the true Christian. People have their own personal reasons for being interested in religion. There are certain things they want and they think that religion can provide them – that is the Judas attitude. The true Christian is one who goes empty-handed, as it were, with an open mind and heart and just listens and receives. Judas never did that. He always had his own point of view, his own interests, and it was to further them that he kept with the disciples. He never really opened himself to receive the message because he was selfish and self-centred.

And there is another great lesson here. Does it not show us the final and complete fallacy and fatuity of thinking anybody can ever be saved or become a Christian merely by teaching or instruction? So many people think that. They say, 'We do not believe in the rebirth, what is needed is good teaching'. But they say that in spite of the case of Judas. Here is a man who for three years received divine instruction through the lips of the blessed Son of God himself, and yet he is 'a son of perdition'. By mere

---

[2] The NIV translates this: '... he was a thief; as keeper of the money bag, he used to help himself to what was put into it.' (Ed.)

teaching and instruction no man can ever be made a Christian. Or take the people who think that the way to make people Christian is to give them a good example, to put them in the right environment and surround them with the right influence. Is that not the kind of thing that is still being taught? Yet here is a man who had spent three years, not only with the apostles, but in the very innermost presence of the Son of God himself, and yet he is the son of perdition. No, example and influence and environment are not enough. The Christian is not merely a man who is trying to imitate the Lord Jesus Christ, for it cannot be done. In Judas we see a man who has every advantage yet he is lost.

Let me therefore sum it all up in these words. If there is one thing in the Scriptures that proves, more conclusively than anything else, the absolute necessity of the rebirth, it is the case of Judas Iscariot. What differentiates the Christian from the non-Christian is not that the Christian lives a better life than he did before, nor that he knows more of the Scriptures, and all these other good things. Judas knew all that and he probably lived a good outward moral life during the three years he was among the disciples. No, what makes a man a Christian is that he is born again, he has received the divine nature, he has indeed become indwelt by the Spirit of the living God. It is this that gives the understanding, and everything that Judas did not have. It was because Judas was never renewed and given the new life that he remained the son of perdition. And here I want to utter a solemn, terrible word. The end of the non-Christian, even though he may be highly religious, is perdition, which means perishing. Though Judas was in the company of the apostles all along, he really belonged to the world, and the fate of the world is to perish. Whatever its appearance may be, its end is destruction, with no hope whatsoever; because it has not truly believed in the name of the only begotten Son of God, it perishes.

This is an unpleasant subject and yet we have to face it, because, in the very centre of this most wonderful prayer, our

Lord had to mention it as a solemn warning. He was not praying for Judas, he was praying for those who were God's people, those who belong to God.

My dear friends, are we *certain* that we belong to God? Do we know that we have received the divine life? Are we born again, and are we sure of it? I warn you in the name of my blessed Saviour, in the light of this teaching, do not rely upon anything but the certain knowledge that you have received life from God. Interest in religion is not enough, interest in Christ is not enough, interest in morality is not enough, membership of the church is not enough – none of these things is enough. Judas seemed to have had them all. The one thing about which we must be absolutely certain is that we are the children of God. If you are, praise him and give yourself anew to him. If you are not certain, then I beseech you, learn the lesson of Judas. Go to the Lord Jesus Christ and tell him that you are uncertain, that you do not know, that you are even doubtful whether you have new life. Tell him the truth about yourself. Cast yourself utterly at his feet and ask him in mercy to look upon you and by his Spirit give you this new life and the blessed assurance that you are born again, that you are indeed his child and his heir, a joint-heir with Christ, and that you truly belong to him.

11

The World and the Devil

And now I am no more in the world, but these are in the world, and I come to thee. Holy Father, keep through thine own name those whom thou hast given me, that they may be one, as we are. While I was with them in the world, I kept them in thy name: those that thou gavest me I have kept, and none of them is lost, but the son of perdition; that the scripture might be fulfilled. And now come I to thee; and these things I speak in the world, that they might have my joy fulfilled in themselves. I have given them thy word; and the world hath hated them, because they are not of the world, even as I am not of the world. I pray not that thou shouldest take them out of the world, but that thou shouldest keep them from the evil (vv. 11–15).

We continue now with our study of our Lord's great plea that God should keep the disciples in his name, the name which he had given to Christ to reveal to them. 'While I was with them in the world,' he says, 'I kept them in thy name', and his prayer is that God will continue to keep them in the name. You notice the urgency of the plea which emphasizes the need of our being kept. We cannot read this prayer without noticing that it was obviously a great burden on our Lord's mind. He was going to leave them in the world, and he was concerned about them, so concerned that though he was going to face the shame and agony and terrible trial of the cross, he really was not thinking about himself, but about them, and about their future. We see this clearly not only in this chapter but also repeatedly in all his

131

teaching at the end of his life. He was, in a sense, almost alarmed about them and thus he offered his urgent plea.

Now this is something which is characteristic of the whole of the New Testament teaching about the Christian and his life in this world. We find in Acts 20 that the apostle Paul had precisely the same concern about the people in the church at Ephesus. He was hurrying up to Jerusalem; he knew that bonds awaited him, and he was quite certain that he was never going to see these people again. So he sent an urgent message to the elders of the church at Ephesus to meet him on the seashore, and there he addressed them. He, again, felt this burden – I know, he said, that you will never see my face again. I cannot come to you any more and teach you as I should like to do, and therefore I want to warn you against certain things. And he proceeded to do that. He told them about the 'grievous wolves' that were ready to attack them, and he added that they would find that even among themselves there were those who were going to rise up and make havoc of the life of the church. The apostle was burdened for these people as he was leaving them, and the last thing he did before he said farewell was to kneel down on the seashore and pray for them. He committed them to God, exactly as our Lord here was committing his disciples and other followers into the hands of his Father. You can find other illustrations of the same concern.

The message for us, therefore, is that the life of the Christian in this world is a life of conflict. The New Testament always, everywhere, gives the impression that all who are Christians are in the midst of a tremendous spiritual battle. Think, for instance, of that great exhortation in Ephesians 6 where Paul exhorts the Christians to 'put on the whole armour of God' in order that they may be able to stand in the evil day. 'For,' he says, 'we wrestle not against flesh and blood, but against principalities, against powers, against the rulers of the darkness of this world, against spiritual wickedness in high places,' or in the heavenlies. Now that is typical and interesting teaching. You cannot read the New Testament without being aware of this kind of tension. The world is the scene of the great battle that is going on between these rival, spiritual forces, and the Christian is involved in all this, of course, because he belongs to the Lord Jesus Christ. The very fact that we belong to Christ means that we immediately become the special targets of the enemies of Christ, those other spiritual forces to whom Paul refers. They are antagonistic to God and his Christ, and, therefore, the moment we belong to God the enemy begins to attack us, not because he is interested in us, but because his one overriding ambition is to mar and destroy God's perfect work. Our Lord knew this and so did Paul and all the apostles. Peter, for instance, puts it like this, 'Be sober, be vigilant; because your adversary the devil, as a roaring lion, walketh about, seeking whom he may devour ...' (1 Pet 5:8). That is the picture, and it is because of this that the need for protection arises.

I wonder whether we are conscious of our position and our condition as Christians? I wonder whether we are conscious of our need to be kept, or whether we are aware of the tremendous spiritual conflict in which we are involved? I ask these questions because I think I know many church members who patently are not aware of this conflict at all and who feel that it is something strange and odd. So I do not hesitate to asssert that one of the most interesting ways of measuring our spiritual understanding and insight is to discover the degree to which we are aware of the fight and the conflict and the position with which we are confronted as Christians in this present evil world. To the extent that we are not aware of it and so not aware of the need for protection, to that extent, I would say, we are simply proclaiming that we are tiros in these matters, and that we are but babes in Christ. The babe never realizes the dangers, everything seems easy and simple and plain, but the more we grow, and the older we get, the more we begin to realize the subtleties and the dangers that confront us. It is exactly the same in the spiritual life and it is the saints, of all people, who have realized most acutely that they are confronted by a mighty, spiritual antagonist. Read the lives of the saints and you will find that they are always aware of this – which is why they spent so much time in prayer. It is the man who realizes his own weakness and the power of the devil, who realizes his need for protection.

Now our Lord here establishes this once and for ever. His great burden under the very shadow of the cross was the condition of these people. He was leaving them and he saw the forces that were marshalling themselves and making ready to swoop upon them and attack them. He saw exactly what was going to take place, and so he pleaded with God to keep them, and to keep them in his name.

And not only that. Our Lord goes on to particularize these forces that are arrayed against us, and they can be summed up under two headings. First of all there is the world itself. In every single one of these verses from verse 11 to verse 15 the world is mentioned, and this is because the disciples are in the world. Indeed the problem arises because that is where he must leave them. Now this does not mean, of course, the physical world, but the world in a spiritual sense, the sense in which the New Testament always uses this expression. It is the mind, the outlook and the whole organization of this present world and scene. 'Love not the world, neither the things that are in the world,' says the apostle John. The Scripture describes the powers and the forces that are opposed to God as 'the world'; it is the realm in which Satan is king, the atmosphere in which the prince of the power of the air rules and reigns. It is the territory of 'the god of this world', everything in life that does not recognize God and submit itself to him.

Now the world manifests itself and its antagonism to the Christian in many ways. Our Lord singles one out here by saying, 'I have given them thy word; and the world hath hated them, because they are not of the world, even as I am not of the world.' He said that many times. He tells his disciples in John 15 that the world will hate them because it hated him and because they are like him and because they belong to him. Our Lord does not argue about this. The world, he says, *will hate you*, and here, in pleading for these people with the Father, he makes the same statement; the world which has hated them will go on hating. This is surely an extraordinary thing. The world hates the Christian. So here again we come across a valuable differentiating point. There are so many things that simulate Christianity in this modern world – indeed there always have been – that it is sometimes very difficult to differentiate between Christianity and a kind of pseudo-Christianity. But this, I think, is one of the best tests. The world never hates the imitation, or the spurious, or the false Christianity, but it always hates the true thing. The world never hates morality, it never hates the merely moral man (which is an interesting point), but it hates the true Christian. You would have thought that if the world hated the one, it would hate the other, but no, the world, in a sense, likes the moral man. It never hates him because it realizes that he is acting in his own strength, and in that way he is paying a compliment to fallen human nature. But the world hated the Son of God himself, and it hates the true saint.

The world hates the true Christian because Christ himself and the true Christian condemn the natural man in a way that nobody else does. Christ and the saint condemn the natural man at his very best, and that is why the world hates him. It is only in Christ and the true Christian that the doctrine of sin is really perceived. The very fact that the Son of God came into this world at all is proof positive that man can never save himself. If man could save himself by his own exertions, the Son of God would never have come. The very fact that he has come proclaims that man at his best and highest will never be good enough. Now the world hates the thought of this because the ultimate trouble with man in sin is his pride, and that is why so often the most moral people have been the ones who have hated the Christ of God most of all. The poor sinner in his rags and filth never hates Christ as much as the good moral man does, the man who only believes in 'uplift' and ideals. He is the man who hates Christ because Christ condemns him. He feels he is better than that other man in the gutter and that he has no need of Christ. Scripture says that 'all have sinned', and he cannot stand the condemnation.

And of course our Lord condemns him in the same way by the cross. The cross proclaims that all are lost and that all are equally under the wrath of God, and the world hates that. Men are so ready to praise the example and the teaching of Christ, but they ridicule his blood, for it is the blood that condemns and what a man cannot endure is the sense of condemnation, the sense of inadequacy, and the sense of failure. Thus it comes to pass that our Lord and his followers are hated by the world. The world says, 'I do not object to religion, but why go so far? Why this separating of yourself from others? I really am not as bad as that after all I confess I am not 100% but ...' and Christ condemns that. He says, 'You are a sinner', and the world hates him for that and it hates his followers. Our Lord's words were of course very soon verified. The spite of the Jews was turned upon the first Christians, and the enmity of the world has continued up to this present time. That is a terrifying thing to say but it is true.

Does the world hate us? I wonder whether it hates us as it hated our Lord? If it does not it is simply because we are very poor Christians. I trust nobody will misunderstand me, I am not saying that a man must try to make himself angular or difficult. Our Lord did not break the bruised reed, or quench the smoking flax. No, it did not hate him because he made himself odd and difficult, it was his sheer purity and holiness, and his teaching that caused the hatred. And it is as true today as it has always been that the nearer we approximate to our Lord the more we experience the hatred of the world. It shows it of course in many ways. It shows it in persecution, which can be open, but which can also be subtle and concealed. It is in an open form in many countries of the world today, and there are people in concentration camps and prisons because the world hates them. But in a different way, there is as much persecution in this country as there is in those other countries. It is the subtle form with which we are all familiar and the man who is a true follower of Christ will inevitably be subjected to it. 'Yea,' says Paul to Timothy, 'and all that will live godly in Christ Jesus shall suffer persecution' (2 Tim 3:12). Let us all examine ourselves.

That is the first thing. The world is opposed and it shows its opposition by means of hatred. But it also has another way of showing it. This is what I would call the Demas way – 'Demas

hath forsaken me, having loved this present world' (2 Tim
4:10). The world does not care very much how it attacks his followers. If by throwing them into prison it can wrest them from
Christ, it will do so, but if that does not work it will try some
other method. 'Demas hath forsaken me' – the love of ease, love
of the things of the world, its wealth, its position, its so-called
pomp and show, the lust of the flesh, the lust of the eye and the
pride of life – how many good men have been ruined by that.
Prosperity can be very dangerous to the soul and the world is
prepared to use that. If direct opposition will not work, it will
pamper us, it will dangle these things before us and thus it will
try to wean us from Christ. So it is not surprising that he prayed
the Father to keep us in his name.

Then another way in which the world does the same thing is
by what may be described as the Barnabas method. We are told
in Acts 15 that a dispute had taken place between Barnabas and
Paul. Barnabas wanted to take his relative John Mark on their
missionary journey but Paul said that he would not have him.
Paul felt that John Mark had let them down and deserted them
when they had taken him on their previous journey and that he
was not, therefore, the man to accompany them. Here we have
worldly relationships such as family relationships interfering in
God's work. It is always something which to me seems very
subtle and pathetic at the same time. You read of men who have
been called by God to do a particular work. Their call has been
quite clear and unmistakable, but then when these men get old
you notice the way they tend to appoint their own sons to carry
on the work and how often it leads to disaster. The point is, of
course, that the God who called the father, does not of necessity
call the son. Indeed I have seen this kind of thing so often that I
become very uneasy when I see it taking place. It is the Barnabas
method – 'John Mark must come, he is my relative.' In other
words, it is the tendency not to judge things in a spiritual way,
but to be influenced by these other considerations.

Indeed, this can show itself in still another way, the way
which James emphasizes when he says, 'Pure religion and undefiled before God and the Father is this, To visit the fatherless

and widows in their affliction, and to keep himself unspotted from the world' (Jas 1:27). It may seem a strange bringing together of two statements, but it is essential that the two should be taken together. It is a right and a good thing to visit the fatherless and the widows, says James, but be very careful that you do not become spotted with the world as you do so. Have we not all, alas, known numbers of men called of God to be prophets and to preach the gospel who have ended as nice, but powerless men, whose congregations have been ruined. They have visited the fatherless and the widows in their affliction, but they have not been careful to keep themselves unspotted from the world. They have been affable and friendly and kind, but they have lost something. It was the world that did it, it came between the man and his calling, between this man and God and his Christ.

There, then, are some of the ways in which the world does this, but our Lord does not stop at mentioning the world. He specifically mentions the evil one – 'I pray not that thou shouldest take them out of the world, but that thou shouldest keep them from the evil' – or 'the evil one' (v. 15). Both renderings, of course, are perfectly true: we pray to be kept from the evil one and the other evil things which belong to the evil one and are prompted by him. In other words, we must see that it is not only the world that is against us, it is also the 'god of this world' behind the world, the devil himself. Our Lord has taught us to pray this in the prayer he taught his disciples: 'Lead us not into temptation, but deliver us from evil' – or the evil one. As I have already reminded you, Peter tells us that this adversary of ours is roaming about like a roaring lion, 'seeking whom he may devour' – he is the devil who is opposed to God's people.

How then does he attack them? Well, sometimes he makes a direct attack on the self, on the person, and there are a great variety of ways in which he does this. I suppose that the commonest way of all is through our pride; he fills us with a sense of elation and self-glorification. Let me give you a perfect illustration of that from Luke 10. Our Lord had sent his disciples out to preach the gospel and to cast out devils and they came back to him full of elation because they said that even the devils were subject to them. Our Lord immediately saw the danger and said to them, 'In this rejoice not, that the spirits are subject unto you; but rather rejoice because your names are written in heaven.' You see, he saw the danger of their heads being turned – as we put it – of their being consumed with self-satisfaction at their success, reporting the results, letting everybody know, and being puffed up with pride. And, of course, this pride leads in turn to self-reliance. We think we are so wonderful and do the work so well that we do not need the Holy Spirit and the power of God. We can do it, so we trust to our organization and all our carnal means and methods, and the devil encourages us in this. He drives us forward in a false, carnal or excessive zeal.

Another way he has, and it is one of his favourite methods, is to make us rush ahead of God. He makes us impatient; we cannot wait for God's time. We are going to do this thing, and we will arrange, we will organize, we will go ahead of God – and the devil is satisfied and well-pleased. Appearing as an angel of light, he encourages us to rely upon ourselves and our own ideas and methods, and thus God's blessing is withheld.

But he is subtle, and sometimes he takes us in, not by puffing us up with pride, nor by encouraging us, but by doing the exact opposite. He fills us with discouragement and doubt or he encourages us in a sense of false modesty. I have seen the devil ruin many a prayer meeting like that. There is a pause in the meeting and if you asked every person who was present why they did not take part, they would say, 'I did not like to push myself forward, I was giving somebody else a chance.' And the prayer meeting is ruined through false, unhealthy pseudo-modesty. He makes us condemn ourselves; he makes us look at some sin which we committed many years ago and he makes us look back at it and feel that we cannot be forgiven. So the result is that we are constantly looking at our failures, and while we are doing that, we are not working for God. We feel that we are altogether unworthy of him; we doubt ourselves and our salvation and we spend the whole of our time examining ourselves.

My dear friends, from the devil's standpoint there is not the slightest difference between being puffed up with pride in yourself or spending the whole of your time condemning yourself. Either way the devil is very well-pleased. Any concentration upon self in any shape or form is always of the devil. Another result, of course, is that while we are looking at ourselves and thinking of ourselves, we are forgetting this name in which our Lord asked his Father to keep us, the name that tells us that all our sins are forgiven and that the blood of Christ still cleanses from all sin and unrighteousness. If that is true, I have no right to look back to that sin; I must turn to the name, and if I feel weak I must remember that God is the almighty Jehovah who has promised not to leave me nor forsake me. So we must not allow the devil to hinder the work of God with a direct attack in one or other of these ways.

Again, he can do it by creating within us a spirit of fear. We read how the devil dealt with Peter and all the disciples immediately after this prayer was offered. Peter, to save his skin, denied his Lord just at the time when his Lord was actually on trial and needed support and help and comfort. Peter denied him and they all forsook him and fled because of a fear of consequences and the desire to avoid pain or persecution. The devil will always encourage that kind of thing and that is why our Lord spoke so often about it. Read Matthew 10 and you will find a long sermon on that very theme – 'Fear not them which kill the body, but are not able to kill the soul: but rather fear him which is able to destroy both soul and body in hell.' Fear takes various forms. For instance we say, 'If I do this, what is going to happen to me, professionally, or in business? Will I get my promotion? Will I be regarded as an odd man out? What is going to happen to my family?' Fear – it is always of the devil and that is why our Lord prayed that we might be kept in the name of God.

Then the devil's second great line of attack is an attack upon the truth, and the Bible is full of warnings about this. The devil attacks the truth by introducing false teaching. That is why, as we read in Acts 20, Paul said what he did to the elders of the Ephesian church. He could see what would happen in Ephesus after his departure. He knew of wolves that were waiting to come in with their false teaching, those men amongst their own number who were out to destroy; the devil was at the back of all that. Read the first epistle of John: it is full of warnings about this – the anti-Christs who had already arisen and were causing havoc in the church. Read in 2 Peter 2 about the people, these 'false teachers', who will insinuate themselves amongst the believers. Read the epistle of Jude with his great exhortation on this theme and all his warnings of the activity of the devil within the life of the church. Is it surprising, then, that our Lord prayed so urgently that his Father would keep his people in his name? He knew that all this was going to come – the devil with his false teaching.

But it is not always bald, false teaching. It is sometimes more subtle, coming in the form of compromise. Of course, if you stand up in a pulpit and say, 'Jesus of Nazareth was only a man, he was not the Son of God', most people would recognize it as not being the true doctrine. But if the preacher does not actually *say* anything wrong, I am afraid that there are often many Christian people who can be entirely taken in by him. It is a subtle compromise which makes a man preach the gospel without any offence in it. He talks about the death of Christ in a way that leads you to pity Christ, and to think that the preacher's picture of the cross is beautiful. But that is because there is no offence of the cross in his preaching, the devil is subtle in this. There are often men who start with a true doctrine but who end with compromise. The offence is taken out of their preaching and out of their gospel. And the same is true of the individual, the Christian member of the church. Oh, very well, we say, for the sake of unity we will not stress that as we used to. For the sake of not offending anybody we will leave out these things and use the things that are generally accepted – compromise. Oh in that way the devil has made havoc of the Christian church during the last hundred years.

And then another way in which he does this is one which I have already mentioned in another connection. He makes us resort to worldly wisdom and worldly methods in order to gain success, and we forget the name. I have no doubt that this came as a real temptation to Paul as he stood outside the city of Corinth. I am sure that he had a fight upon that road. The devil would turn to him and say, 'These people like philosophy, and rhetoric. You know all that stuff – give it to them, and they will like you, and you will have a great church.' But Paul tells the Corinthians in his first letter to them, 'I determined not to know any thing among you, save Jesus Christ, and him crucified.' He would not resort to any such methods. He kept himself to the simplicity that is in Christ, and the purity of the message and the purity of presenting the message. And this is something which he constantly repeats.

But lastly, I would remind you that the devil attacks the truth by means of encouraging schisms and divisions in the church. I am not going to stay with this matter now, because we have to come back to it when we deal with the great plea for unity. Let me just put it like this here. The cause of schism is that men and women have put something other than the truth into the position of truth. They put in the supreme position things that belong to the circumference, and the moment you do that there will be schism. Was that not the trouble with the church at Corinth? Paul deals with this in a very remarkable way in his first letter to the Corinthians. The Corinthians had been putting personality in the position of principle, saying, 'I am of Paul', or 'I am of Apollos' (1 Cor 1:12). Instead of Christ and his gospel, they put a particular preacher in the centre and therefore there was division. Again, take spiritual gifts – they were talking and arguing about which was the superior gift of the Spirit, and because some put miracles etc. in the centre, there was schism, and Paul condemns it in chapter 12, for it is dividing the body of Christ, and the devil encourages that. If he can lead us astray by putting any particular thing in the central position of our faith – a denomination or a man, a cause or a particular aspect of truth – rather than Christ himself, he will always encourage us to do so, and thereby he attacks us and divides us, and he wounds the body.

All these things, as we have seen, are simply meant to draw us away from God and his Christ; they are simply methods by which the devil tries to spoil the work of God. He did it at creation, at the beginning, he has done it ever since and he is trying to do it with the church today. God made everything and saw that it was good, and the devil came in and spoilt it all. It is no new thing; the devil is out with all his might and main to mar and to wreck and to ruin the work of Christ, and our one and greatest comfort is that our blessed Lord not only knows that, but has committed the church to his Father and has prayed and is praying the Father to keep us, to keep us in his own name, that we may be saved from the world and the flesh and the devil. Let us meditate about these things, let us realize the danger, let us realize the subtlety. Let us never allow Satan to gain the advantage over us. Let us be aware of his devices so that we may withstand him, steadfast in the faith, and thus, by the power of God in Christ through the Holy Spirit, be made more than conquerors.

12

God's Perfect Will

*I pray not that thou shouldest take them out of the world, but that
thou shouldest keep them from the evil (v. 15).*

As we start on this final study, let me remind you of our analysis
of this second section of our Lord's great high priestly prayer
which he prays as he is under the very shadow of the cross. Our
Lord, having prayed for himself, proceeds to pray for those he
is leaving behind in this world of time, and we find he gives various reasons for praying for them. And so we have this wonderful description of the Christian, found especially in verses 6, 7
and 8 but also running right through the entire paragraph. Then
we come to the petitions which he offers for them. The first petition is that God should keep them – 'Holy Father, keep through
thine own name those whom thou hast given me' – though they
are in the world – 'that they may be one, as we are.' He says that
while he was with them he kept them all but the son of perdition
– Judas – that the Scriptures might be fulfilled. And now he
commits them to his Father and prays God urgently to keep
them.

Our Lord asks his Father to keep them because of the world
which, he says, hates them: 'I have given them thy word; and
the world hath hated them, because they are not of the world,
even as I am not of the world.' The world is opposed to the
Christian and we have considered the various ways in which it
manifests this opposition and hatred. If there is one thing,

surely, that is emphasized constantly in the Scriptures, in the Old Testament and the New, it is that the Christian is a stranger and a pilgrim in this world. He is different. He does not belong to the world; he is in it but not of it. His mentality and outlook, his whole central position, are entirely different from that of the world, and it is a fact that the world hates him because of that. As our Saviour has already told these men: 'The servant is not greater than his Lord' (Jn 13:16); 'If they have called the master of the house Beelzebub, how much more shall they call them of his household?'; 'Ye shall be hated of all men for my name's sake' (Mt 10:25, 22). That is why, of course, there is a great conflict going on in this world between unseen spiritual forces, a great and mighty conflict between God and all who belong to him, and the devil and all who belong to him. And the world is controlled by the devil; he is the god of this world; he rules in the midst of men and women who belong to the world. He is 'the spirit that now worketh in the children of disobedience,' says the apostle Paul in Ephesians 2:2. The devil hates God and the Lord Jesus Christ with all his might and being and power, and he hates all who belong to him, and the result is that all who are controlled by the devil are of necessity antagonistic to those who belong to God.

There is no question at all about this. The life of our Lord proves it, the lives and experience of the apostles prove it, and the lives of the saints throughout the centuries prove it. To the extent to which a man is godly and living the life God would have him live, to that extent he will experience malignity and opposition in the world. So our Lord prays to God to keep them against all that. And he likewise prays that God should keep them from the evil one and from evil in all its forms, however it is manifested under the power of the devil. Our Lord's prayer is that God should keep us from the evil, keep us, as it were, out of the clutches of the evil one. As we saw, the devil comes to us and attacks us in various ways, filling us with pride and elation, or depressing us with despair and he works and plays upon us between these two extremes. He knows us all. He is well aware of our every mood and state and condition, he can even affect our physical frame and body and by such things can depress us and hold us down. There is no end to the ways in which the devil in all his subtlety and power is able to attack the children of God, and so our Lord prays that we may be kept.

But we must now go on to consider how it is that God keeps us. In what ways does our Lord ask his Father to do this? The first answer to that question is here in verse 15, and strangely enough we find that it is a negative answer. Now it may surprise us that our Lord should specifically have uttered this negative thought and petition. He says, I do *not* ask you to take them out of the world, that is not my request. And people are often perplexed at this. Indeed it is often the cause of much questioning and misunderstanding.

I suppose that ultimately the sin of which we are all most frequently guilty is the sin of asking certain questions which we would never ask if we were truly mature Christians. Because of our frailty and unbelief we say that there are certain things we do not and cannot understand. Here, surely, is one such question and it is one of the most common of all. Why is it that when we become Christians God does not immediately take us out of the world, especially in view of the state of the world in which we live? But consider what we are told here. If ever anyone experienced the malignity of the world our Lord did, but we see him specifically praying that the disciples should not be taken out of it, even though he knew exactly the kind of world it was. He saw it and knew it, and saw through it, in a way no one else has ever done. He knew its persecution and its scorn and its derision and all its opposition. He knew all about that, for he had experienced it, and yet, though he knew that and though he knew the weakness and the frailty of these men, he did not ask God to take them out of the world. He left them in the world knowing all about what was going to meet them and to confront them. Now that often puzzles many people. They wonder why it is that we are not immediately taken to heaven and to glory when we become Christians – and of course this is one of the questions which we ask far too often.

Another question that is asked is: why is it that when we

become Christians we are not immediately made perfect and sinless? We argue that God has power to do this. We know that God the Holy Spirit can do this, for we know that ultimately we shall be presented faultless and blameless in the presence of God. Therefore, we argue, if God has this power, and if God can completely and entirely sanctify us from all sin, why does he not do it immediately? Why, when we are born again, are we not completely delivered at once from the old man and nature and everything that belongs to sin and its polluting effect? Why are we not immediately made entirely sanctified and holy? You have often asked that question – it is one of those questions which fall into this self-same category. Why are we not entirely taken out of the world? Why are we left in this struggle and in this life?

Or take another question. Since the Lord Jesus Christ dealt with sin upon the cross and in his resurrection, why are we not automatically delivered from all the consequences of sin? As it has been dealt with finally and conquered once and for ever, why is it that its evil consequences are not removed? I refer to things such as sickness and illness and disease which are undoubtedly the consequences of sin and of the fall. Why were they not all immediately taken away? Why do we still inherit these things – the frailties, the weaknesses, the infections and all these diseases to which we are still subject in this world of time? Since sin was dealt with in the matter of guilt and so on, why was not all this removed? You notice I am putting it in question form. There are people who teach that this has been done, but that is an error and a heresy, Scripture itself makes that perfectly clear. I put it in the form of questions, and the people who ask these questions often go on to the error and the heresy.

There is also the fact of death – that is a consequence of sin. If man had not sinned death would not have entered into the world. But God has dealt with sin, so why are we still subject to death? Why does it not come to pass that people who become Christians no longer see death – why do they have to go through that? Why was death not taken right away, once and for ever, as a consequence of Calvary and the resurrection?

Or again, to ask still another of these questions: why should there have been this terrible long interval between Christ's first and second coming? If it is God's plan and purpose that Christ should come back to rid the world of all evil and sin, and conquer death, why this long interval? Nearly 2,000 years have gone and still we have this evil world and we are still confronted by all these terrible things. We believe that he is coming, but why did he not come at once? That is the kind of question we ask, and that leads us right back to a prior question, namely, why was there such a long interval between the fall of man and the first coming of Christ? That is a great question which we often put like this: we believe that even before God made the world and created man, it was his purpose to save the world. Why, then, did he allow 4,000 years to pass between the fall of man and the coming of Christ? Why all this long degraded history with its record of apparent failure and frustration? Why all the long story of the years? Why didn't he send Christ at once? These are the questions we ask and they all arise out of these words which we are considering here: 'I pray not that thou shouldest take them out of the world ...' Why not? Why should we be left in it to suffer and endure? Why is the second coming so long delayed when the whole world will be turned again into a state of paradise?

These are the questions and it is vital, therefore, that we should answer them. Now I am tempted to say that in reality there is only one answer, and that if we were what we ought to be as Christian people, this answer would be enough. The one fundamental, final answer is that it is God's way, it is the way which God has determined and the way that God has planned. And all that I shall say now is really going to lead up to that – that is the beginning and that is the end, and the position of faith is one in which man is content with God's way though he does not understand it. In other words, I really am suggesting that we should never ask these questions at all. It is impudence and impertinence on the part of feeble man to do so. We should never ask such questions because our attitude of faith should be that what God did and what God does is always right and that there is no need for us to ask the reason why. It is for us to believe and accept and above all to submit to it.

However, I believe that Scripture entitles us to give supplementary answers and it is here that we see the mercy and the condescension of God. He does not merely leave us with the words, 'That is my will and you must accept it.' He stoops to our weakness and gives us glimpses into his great and inscrutable reasons. He enables us, while still here on earth and still in our imperfection, to have some kind of inkling of what we shall see perfectly when we arrive in glory. So let us proceed to consider some of these subsidiary or supplementary answers to the question as to why God does these things in this way.

Now it is always good to start with a fact, so let me begin by saying that the great fact here is that God acts as he does because it is his will. I wonder if you have ever noticed that there are three recorded requests in Holy Scripture about which we are told that God did not grant the request? These were from three remarkable and saintly men and the interesting thing is that it was the same petition each time, it was a prayer to the effect that they should die and that they should be taken out of the world.

The first was Moses. Moses had been chosen as God's leader among the people and here he was struggling with this recalcitrant mob. He had gone up to meet God on the mountain and in his absence the people had made a golden calf and were worshipping it. Moses became frantic and said to God, in effect, 'Will you grant me my petition? If not, take me out of this life because I would sooner be dead.' His prayer was not granted.

The second was that mighty man Elijah, one of the most outstanding characters in Scripture, the man who greatly appeals to everybody because he could stand alone and defy a king and a collection of eight hundred and fifty false prophets. But in 1 Kings 19 you will see this self-same man sitting under a juniper tree thoroughly miserable and unhappy. The man who defied the whole world yesterday is today running away from a woman. He does not understand things and his prayer to God is that he should be taken out of it all. He wants to die but God does not grant him his request.

The third case is the prophet Jonah. Poor Jonah! He knew exactly the state of affairs in Nineveh. It was a terrible, sinful city and Jonah wanted it to be blotted out. God sent him to preach repentance to that city but to his amazement God said he would withhold his judgement – and Jonah did not like it. He felt that God was against him and he wanted to die. But he was not taken out of the world and he did not die. So here are three notable saints of God each of whom prayed the same prayer but God did not grant their request.

We are thus confronted by this great fact and, though we have to say that ultimately we do not know the complete reason, we do recognize that in the wisdom of God this is not his way of dealing with his people. 'I pray not that thou shouldest take them out of the world' – but, why not? Well, I think that we can feel after certain answers to that question. Why is our Lord thus concerned that God should not take the disciples out of the world? A part of the answer is that if they were removed like that, who would be left to preach the gospel to the world? Indeed, our Lord says that quite specifically – 'As thou hast sent me into the world, even so have I also sent them into the world.' God sent the Son into the world to preach the truth and to present the gospel and to make a way of salvation and now, as he is going out of the world, he is sending them into it and leaving the message with them. They are going to be the preachers, in their lives as well as with their words – they are going to represent him. As we have seen, he says, 'I am glorified in them.' Therefore they cannot ask to be taken out of the world because they are being sent there to perform this specific task.

It is so tragic to notice how often we forget that, and it is because we forget that as Christians we are God's and Christ's representatives in this world that we sometimes ask to be taken out of it. But we have a great and mighty and noble task to perform. We are the salt of the earth, we are the light of the world shining brightly amidst the gloom and despair and holding forth the word of life – if only we always realized that this is our calling and our business! If I may put it like this it may help us to understand. What if our Lord himself, when he was in this world, had turned to God and said, 'Why do you send me? I do not want to stay here, it is such a terrible, sinful, evil, dark world, let me come back to you, take me out of it'? But he never did – no, he had come deliberately to do the work, to perform the task. He knew why he had come, so he says here to the disciples, 'I did the work and you are to do the same.' That is sufficient reason in and of itself for not desiring to be taken out of the world.

Then the second reason I deduce is that there is no doubt at all but that we are left in this world because it is part of the process of our being perfected. We need to be perfected, a gradual work has to be done in all of us even after we are born again and regenerated, and God, I believe, leaves us in this world in order that we may be so perfected and prepared for him. We all need to be humbled, to be brought down to the dust. It is obviously very clear that the fact that a man is a Christian does not mean that he is entirely delivered from pride and conceit, self-centredness and self-interest; you sometimes see these things in a rampant form even among Christian people. We must be delivered from all that, and if the positive truth of the gospel does not deliver us from it, then God has another way of doing it, and he humbles us by such things as disappointment, failure, weakness, or illness.

I believe that the apostle Paul is referring to this in 2 Corinthians 12. He had had a great struggle over it. There was a danger that he might be exalted and lifted up because of the revelations that had been given to him, and God had had to deal with him by giving him what he calls 'a thorn in the flesh', which humbled him and kept him down. Paul admits it, and it is true of every one of us. We live in this world and we sometimes think that no temptation is ever going to affect us. We have risen above it – we are above and beyond these things! We are even insulted at the word that says, 'Wherefore let him that thinketh he standeth take heed lest he fall.' So, for our humbling and our good, God leaves us to ourselves. Then the devil takes advantage and we fall, down to the very dust, and it is there that God says to us, 'whom the Lord loveth he chasteneth' (Heb 12:6).

He also tries us, tries our faith to see what we are made of, as it were, and it is all part of our development. We start as children and as babes. At first everything seems to be so easy in the Christian life, but a time comes when we realize that it is not. There are many Christian people who look back with longing to the days of their conversion, but they are absolutely wrong in doing so. It is a terrible thing for us to say, 'Where is the blessedness I knew when first I saw the Lord?' We should never say that, and Cowper was a deeply depressed man when he wrote those words. But we, too, tend to say it because we rather like a life of ease; we are like spoilt children, but, thank God, our heavenly Father does not deal with us like that. Times come when we are confronted by problems and difficulties. I have heard of and known men in the ministry who, when they start, are given texts and sermons as gifts from God, but they very often find that as they go on they have to struggle much more than they did at the beginning. They have become men, and are no longer children, and it is right that they should know the difficulties. Mr Spurgeon said he found he had to work much harder in the ministry, making and preparing his sermons, when he was older than he did when he was the famous boy preacher at the age of seventeen or eighteen. It is right, it is part of this process. In other words, God has to show us ourselves, he has to reveal to us our own limitations; the babe in Christ may be happy, but he is very ignorant and he has a lot to learn. Thus, you see, a part of the process of our being made fit for heaven and glory is carried out through our being left in the world and not taken out of it.

But let me give you some other reasons which are more important. We have looked at reasons taken from our side, but there are many reasons from God's side. It is only as we are left in this world in this way that God's marvels and glories are really displayed in us and through us. I suppose that in the last analysis there is nothing that so displays the wonder of God's power than the way in which he can keep people like us as his own in this world. Have you ever thought of it like that? Have you considered the power that is necessary to keep a Christian as a Christian in this world of time, surrounded by suggestions and temptations and everything that is calculated to get him down? I would say that it is a miracle. It is a manifestation of the supernatural power of God that a Christian ever arrives in heaven at all. God leaves us in this world and shows that he has the power and the might to keep us and to hold us and to perfect that which he has commenced in us. It is a display of God's power which nothing else produces.

It also shows us his long-suffering and patience. Can you read the Old Testament without being impressed by these facets of his character? I like the verse that puts it like this – 'And about the time of forty years suffered he their manners in the wilderness' (Acts 13:18). And what a bad set of manners they were! Oh how they ill-treated God and ignored his patience, and it is equally true of us. Though we are Christians, what poor Christians we are! But how patient God is with us and how amazing his long-suffering as he listens to our questions and tolerates us. And so, while leaving us in this world, he shows the fulness and the many-sidedness of his salvation and its completeness. In Ephesians 3:10 Paul talks of the 'manifold wisdom of God', and what a perfect description that is – many-sided, variegated. You do not know what you want, but you will always find that Christ comes to you and meets you just where you are. And thus it comes to pass that as we live in this world with its trials and troubles and perplexities and problems, we come to know God in a way that we could never know him were it not that we have to go through these things. Do you not find that he is ever surprising you; that you are always making some new discovery, arriving at some fresh knowledge of his grace, because of some peculiar circumstance in which you have been placed? You have had some new experience and God has met you there in a way he has never met you before, and so you have come to know him better. He leaves us here in the world, therefore, partly to display to us the riches of his grace and the manifold character of his loving kindness and his mercy.

Those are some of the reasons, but I want to end on a practical note, and so we will consider the practical application of all this by drawing certain deductions from this great doctrine that we are considering together. The first must be that all attempts at delivering ourselves or removing ourselves from this world must be wrong. I am not here speaking about suicide (about which we would all agree) but about monasticism. Men try to deliver themselves out of this world and all its problems and trials, not only by committing suicide, but also by segregating themselves from the world and becoming anchorites and monks and hermits. The whole idea of monasticism, it seems to me, is a blank contradiction of this prayer of our Lord. It is an attempt to avoid all these truths that we have been considering together, so it must be wrong. It is unscriptural.

Moreover it seems to me that it is a complete denial of James 1:27 – 'To visit the fatherless and widows ... and to keep himself unspotted from the world.' In other words, these people want to keep themselves unspotted from the world by going into a cell or a monastery and by having a wall around them and keeping right away from the world. Not at all! We keep ourselves unspotted from the world while we are sweeping floors or going about the ordinary walks of life. Though we are in the world, we still keep ourselves unspotted from it; that is God's way, not by monasticism.

Another thing of which monasticism is obviously guilty is that it tends to externalize sin, regarding it as something that exists in the physical organization of life. It fails to realize that it is something that is within, in the realm of the spirit and the inner man. I think that many monks have discovered that even though they have left the world, the world is inside them and the world is with them in the monastery. A further fallacy, of course, is to regard what they call 'the religious life' as a vocation; you become a monk and you 'take up' the religious life as it were. Now I defy anybody to show me that teaching anywhere in Scripture. Rather, it is a blank contradiction of what the Bible teaches, because we are meant to live *in* the world: 'I pray not that thou shouldest take them out of the world, but that thou shouldest keep them from the evil.' The monastic view is a complete fallacy in that respect.

And the final fallacy is that it means that they are trusting to their own efforts. They believe that by going out of the world and giving themselves to nothing but prayer and fasting and good works, they find God. But you never can. They are trusting to their own life and power instead of trusting to the power of God to keep them in the world. In other words, monasticism is eventually a lack of faith in God's power. It is as good as saying that the power of God is not enough, you have to segregate yourself. If you stay in the world you become an ordinary Christian; if you want to become an extraordinary Christian, you must become a 'saint' and enter into this 'vocation'. The teaching of Scripture is that the power of God is such that he can keep a man unspotted even in 'a hell on earth'. He can keep him in the midst of it all; and not to believe that, and to think that you have to do it in other ways, is to have a lack of faith in God's power. So we must never seek to remove ourselves from the world.

My second deduction is that God's way is not to take us out of the difficulties and the trials, nor to avoid them. His way is to enable us, and to strengthen us, so that we can go through them with heads erect and undefeated, more than conquerors in them and over them. And that is a wonderful thing.

My next deduction is that we must never grumble at our lot, nor ask these doubting questions. We must rather believe that there is always a purpose in these trials, if we can but see it; we must believe that God has laid this thing upon us and that he has left us in this situation in order that we may show forth his glory. The disciples were left in the world to do that, and you and I can be certain that whatever we may be passing through at this moment is a part of God's plan and purpose for us to show forth his glory. The world may not recognize you, it may ignore and dismiss you, and others may get all that they want from the world. Do not worry about it, Christ knew something similar. The saints have experienced the same thing: 'Woe unto you, when all men shall speak well of you!' (Lk 6:26). Yes, 'And all that will live godly in Christ Jesus shall suffer persecution' (2 Tim 3:12). All is well, you are fulfilling the glory of God as you go through that trial. Paul came to see that about the thorn in the flesh. 'All right,' he says, in effect, 'I asked you three times to remove it but you are leaving it. I see now that your glory is going to be shown through me. Very well, I will glory in this infirmity. I will stop asking you to take it away. It is really when I am weak that your power is made manifest in me and through me.' So we must never grumble. We must gladly accept what he allows, and remember that we are fulfilling the glory of God.

I can put that still more strongly. We must never desire peace and ease in this world. As the hymn says:

> Shrink not Christian, will ye yield,
> Will ye quit the painful field,
> Will ye flee in danger's hour,
> Know ye not your Captain's power?
> *H.K. White*
> *F.S. Colquhoun*

Oh we must never 'quit the painful field' or 'flee in danger's hour'. We must never change our position or go out of the situation simply because it is difficult. It is in the difficult situations that God manifests his power. Now it may be God's will for you to change your position. That is all right as long as it is *God's* will for you; but never take the decision yourself simply because things are difficult. Never hand in your resignation because things are going against you. Never come out of anything simply because it is problematical. Stay there until God moves you. He leaves his people in the world; he does not take them out of it.

And that leads me to my last point, which is that in the midst of all these situations and problems we must always look to him and to his power; we must always look to the ultimate that is destined. We know we are going on to glory – 'We have a building of God, an house not made with hands, eternal in the heavens' (2 Cor 5:1). So, whatever may be happening here, keep your eye on that, hold on to it. You know that he has a purpose in leaving you where you are, but you know, too, that you are going on. Keep your eye on him and on that for which you are destined. And if you do that, you will be able to put into practice my last exhortation – let us therefore live every moment of our lives to the full. Never let us waste a second of God's time in asking these foolish, unnecessary questions, in grumbling or in complaining. Having settled this great question in principle, once and for ever, let us never ask it again, but let us take every moment and live it to the maximum. Let us manifest the praises of Christ and of God every split second of our lives, redeeming the time, and clutching at the opportunities.

Look at it like this. Instead of saying, 'Why does God leave me in this world? Why is he leaving me here for another five, ten, or twenty years?' Rather say this: I have another five, ten, twenty years to manifest his praises, to tell his sinful world about him and I am going to take every opportunity I can to do that. Time is passing, it is short, there is so much to be done and so little time in which to do it. So I will live my life to the full and to the maximum, thanking him that he has counted me worthy to fulfil my station in life as his servant, thanking him that Christ has ever sent me, as God the Father sent him, to do these things in the world. I see myself, therefore, as an imitator of Christ, as a re-enactor of the life of Christ.

Yes, let me rise to the height to which the apostle Paul rose in Colossians 1. He said that the afflictions of Christ were being brought up to the full in his body. Paul was making up that which remained of the sufferings of Christ and he regarded that as the greatest privilege that he was allowed in this life and world. He meant by that, that Christ had left him here as his representative, to be a kind of Christ-man, to be living the Christ-like life to the glory of God the Father.

'I pray not that thou shouldest take them out of the world.' Can you say 'Amen' to that? Let us seek to do that and let us thank him that he has sufficient confidence in us and in the power of his Father to leave us even in a world like this, knowing that he can keep us. And in the meantime let us ask him to enable us to serve him and to tell forth his praise and his glory in the world. Amen.